Qualitative Research
nd Theory Development

SAGE has been part of the global academic community since 1965, supporting high quality research and learning that transforms society and our understanding of individuals, groups, and cultures. SAGE is the independent, innovative, natural home for authors, editors and societies who share our commitment and passion for the social sciences.

Find out more at: **www.sagepublications.com**

Qualitative Research and Theory Development

MYSTERY AS METHOD

Mats Alvesson and Dan Kärreman

Los Angeles | London | New Delhi
Singapore | Washington DC

© Mats Alvesson and Dan Kärreman 2011

First published 2011

Apart from any fair dealing for the purposes of
research or private study, or criticism or review, as
permitted under the Copyright, Designs and Patents
Act, 1988, this publication may be reproduced, stored
or transmitted in any form, or by any means, only with
the prior permission in writing of the publishers, or in
the case of reprographic reproduction, in accordance
with the terms of licences issued by the Copyright
Licensing Agency. Enquiries concerning reproduction
outside those terms should be sent to the publishers.

SAGE Publications Ltd
1 Oliver's Yard
55 City Road
London EC1Y 1SP

SAGE Publications Inc.
2455 Teller Road
Thousand Oaks, California 91320

SAGE Publications India Pvt Ltd
B 1/I 1 Mohan Cooperative Industrial Area
Mathura Road
New Delhi 110 044

SAGE Publications Asia-Pacific Pte Ltd
33 Pekin Street #02-01
Far East Square
Singapore 048763

Library of Congress Control Number: 2010938870

British Library Cataloguing in Publication data

A catalogue record for this book is available from the British Library

ISBN 978-0-85702-323-0
ISBN 978-0-85702-324-7 (pbk)

Typeset by C&M Digitals (P) Ltd., Chennai, India
Printed by CPI Antony Rowe, Chippenham, Wiltshire
Printed on paper from sustainable resources

CONTENTS

PREFACE

One of the greatest challenges for social science today is to say something novel and interesting. Today's conventional wisdom is founded on a mountain of established knowledge and there seems to be a broadly shared perception of a lack of new and exciting ideas. Most methodologies are more preoccupied with rigour, procedure, technique and empirical precision than imagination and creative thinking. This often leads to empirical description, careful and cautious analysis, and rather limited theoretical development. In this book we emphasize how empirical studies can be used to come up with unexpected theoretical ideas and lines of thinking. We hope to contribute to a rethinking of empirical social science, particularly within a qualitative tradition, and to inspire less predictable and more exciting theoretical work triggered by empirical material offering inspiration and challenges to established theory.

We are grateful to our colleagues in our organization studies research group at Lund University, especially Stefan Sveningsson, who we have worked with intensively over the years. We are also grateful to John Van Maanen, for excellent feedback and support in the work with the paper Constructing Mystery (published in Academy of Management Review, 2007), in which we first published some of the key ideas of this book.

THE USE OF EMPIRICAL MATERIAL
FOR THEORY DEVELOPMENT

For social scientists, empirical work is one – if not the only – core activity. At the same time, theoretical knowledge is often seen as the most interesting, valuable and prestigious part of a scientific study. It is also broadly seen as the most difficult element to add. The academic reader of a PhD or a reviewer of a research paper will often find the lack of a theoretical contribution one of the greatest shortcomings. It is not so difficult to produce a description of what people do and say through interviews, observations and other methods, but to continue beyond that and suggest insights, concepts, explanations and other 'deeper' aspects offering a more abstract theoretical understanding that goes beyond the relevance of a particular case or sample studied is not so easy. The empirical and theoretical elements are not always engaged in a productive interplay. This is the starting point for this book and we hope to offer some ideas on how this interplay can be accomplished in a creative, challenging, and novel way.

How can empirical studies contribute to the development of theory? According to the conventional wisdom in social science, two basic approaches are available: deduction and induction. Most researchers would still probably adopt a nomothetic approach, thus emphasizing the importance of the deduction of theoretical ideas from earlier knowledge, the formulation of hypotheses, and the testing of these as key ingredients (c.f. Freese, 1980; see also Popper, 1963; 1972). Empirical tests are used either to verify theories, as neo-positivists would put it, or to refute them, as Popper and his followers frame it. Inductivist approaches such as grounded theory (Glaser & Strauss, 1967; Strauss & Corbin, 1994) and many versions of so-called case study research (Eisenhardt, 1989; Yin, 1984) would emphasize the building of theory based on data. Either way, both inductivist and deductivist approaches share a belief in a clear separation of theory and data and a deep seated trust in the capacity of data to inform and correct theory building. They also share a strong belief in premeditated process and both downplay the subjectivity of the researcher.

The case study approach could serve as an illustration for our point. Although Robert Yin is by far the most well-known advocate of the case study approach we will pay particular attention to Kathleen Eisenhardt's (1989) take on the capacity for theory development in the case study approach. Eisenhardt suggests that theory development here proceeds through distinct steps: a tentative formulation of research questions (with as little theoretical baggage included as possible); the selection of cases; the crafting of instruments and protocols; an engagement with the field; analyzing within-case data; searching for cross-case patterns (if multiple cases are researched); shaping hypotheses; enfolding literature; and reaching closure. She also stresses that these moves typically follow one another in an iterative fashion. One would expect at lot of travelling back and forth between stages during research and that this movement is critical for the development of new ideas and insights. In addition, Eisenhardt stresses the inductive character of the theory development process. Theory emerges through intimate contact with empirical materials, and through the frictions and tension between and within various data sets.

She argues that this also leads to one of the biggest strengths with theory development through the case study approach. Since a case study typically leads to rich and messy data sets, these data sets are rife with contradiction and paradox. This makes it possible to juxtapose conflicting evidence, thus freeing up the curious mind to rethink the relationships between the data points. Eisenhardt argues that this increases the potential for new and creative theory:

> That is, attempts to reconcile evidence across cases, types of data, and different investigators, and between cases and literature increase the likelihood of creative reframing into a new theoretical vision. Although a myth surrounding theory building from case studies is that the process is limited by investigators' preconceptions, in fact, just the opposite is true. This constant juxtaposition of conflicting realities tends to 'unfreeze' thinking, and so the process has the potential to generate theory with less researcher bias than theory built from incremental studies or arm-chair, axiomatic deduction. (Eisenhardt, 1989: 546)

She also claims that theory generated from case studies is likely to lead to theory that can be measured and be proven false. The idea here is that since theory emerges from empirical settings it always is rooted in concrete realities and eventualities, which means that it in a sense it is already operationalized and also is less likely to be immunized from falsification. Data will keep the speculative mind in check. Eisenhardt believes as well that theory generated from case studies is likely to be empirically valid. Again, the intimate relationship between data and theory almost guarantees that theory reflects underlying realities. Data, or evidence, will provide a compass that can keep the theory generation process on course.

Yin and Eisenhardt make a strong case for using case studies to generate theory. We would agree with this. Case studies, when properly designed, will be helpful for theory-building purposes for a variety of reasons, but most importantly because they provide a strong potential for a certain thickness of description. Properly executed case studies generate an abundance of empirical material that is almost certain to challenge established assumptions and perspectives. We also think that Yin and Eisenhardt are mostly right about the advantages of case studies. However, we would beg to differ on how case studies can facilitate theory generation. It is clear that both Yin and Eisenhardt have a strong belief in the robust nature of data. This, they both claim, is the big advantage of theory generation from case studies. Data will navigate the process and provide well-grounded and robust theory that has a strong empirical validity. Theory will provide an insight into the complexities and intricacies of empirical reality. In this sense, Yin and Eisenhardt use theory to resolve data, hence the resumed lack of application range.

In this respect inductivists like Eisenhardt and Yin (and Glaser and Strauss), who would claim theory is to be developed through sifting through data, are no different from deductivists who would see theory emerging through the accumulation of verified (or corroborated) hypothesizing. These views of social science are in many ways different, but both rely on data as the central element in social research. Theory is supposed to 'fit' data – either by design, where a lack of fit should lead to rejections or revisions of a theory, or by default, where theory is understood as emerging from data. Theory and data are thus seen as 'external', two different entities that can and should be related while still being recognized as separate.

In this book we shall suggest adopting a different approach. In particular, we would wish to highlight the usefulness of empirical material for theory development through recognizing the fusion of theory and empirical material in the research construction process. We would emphasize the potential of empirical material as a resource for developing theoretical ideas *through the active mobilization and problematization of existing frameworks*. In particular, we shall point to the ways empirical material can be used to facilitate and encourage critical reflection: to enhance our ability to challenge, rethink and illustrate theory. This approach recognizes the constructed nature of empirical material and 'proofs' (Astley, 1985; Denzin & Lincoln, 2005; Shotter, 1993; Shotter & Gergen, 1994; Steier, 1991). It assumes that something is going on out there in reality and there may be better or worse ways of addressing this reality that can be more or less backed up by what might appear to be evidence.

However, it also takes seriously the view that frameworks, pre-understandings and vocabularies are central in producing particular versions of the world. 'Data' in social science are seldom so strong or clear-cut that a researcher can claim to have produced unproblematic knowledge about how complex social reality looks or operates. This is not an excuse for not taking empirical material seriously, but perhaps often to do so in an open-minded and humble way. We would propose a relaxation of the emphasis on 'data' and a greater interest in the contribution of how 'data' are constructed for the benefit of theoretical reasoning (c.f. Sutton & Staw, 1995).

Some time ago, 'empirical' research frequently meant that one could assume an independent reality out there which could be perceived and measured through indications of this reality, i.e. data. Through the careful design of procedures, the collection and processing of data based on this design and the subsequent analysis of these, empirical research could say yes or no to various hypotheses about the chunk of reality targeted for study. Nowadays, it would be seen in many social science camps as old-fashioned, intolerant, and theoretically and philosophically unsophisticated to favour this idea. The label of positivism – as currently broadly defined (or not defined, but used) – invites all sorts of pejorative comments. During recent times, there have been more varied views on what constitutes empirical research, making the meaning of this activity quite vague. Reading texts of all kinds, for example, could constitute undertaking empirical research for some people.

But typically, 'empirical research' refers to taking a strong interest in gathering or constructing empirical material that says something about what goes on out there – in the social life existing outside of the research practices of academics or available texts. Even the increasing number of people in social science who are skeptical to the possibility of the 'collection' and processing of data in order to say yes or no to various hypothesis and theories will often take an interest in empirical work. In many forms of qualitative studies (e.g. in grounded theory) the assumption is that data, carefully processed, can guide the researcher to understand specific phenomena and to develop theory (Glaser & Strauss, 1967; Strauss & Corbin, 1994).[1] In interpretive work it is assumed that we can access and study social reality through indications of the meanings and symbolic interactions that are viewed as crucial elements in social communities. Even though postmodernism give strong reasons for being more careful and modest about such enterprises than previously, it would be remiss of us not to be interested in what we can learn from empirical work.

The key point of this book is to suggest a framework and vocabulary for thinking about theory development that is inspired by empirical studies and different from conventional views of building on data associated with grounded theory and other 'dataistic' approaches. We would thus emphasize the creative and imaginative constructions of empirical material. Rather than assuming that 'data', like a signpost, point in a specific direction, 'data' read as empirical material make a variety of readings possible and may also make different knowledge results possible. Rather than asking and checking if there is a data-theory fit, we ask and explore if empirical material can encourage the challenging and rethinking of established theory and thus inspire novel lines of theory development.

Questioning the Faith in Data

This great faith in data and empirical inquiry as a cornerstone in knowledge development has been challenged by a multitude of intellectual streams during recent years. A powerful example is what may be referred to as 'non-objective' *interpretivist* perspectives. These put an emphasis on how pre-understanding, paradigm and metaphor can pre-structure our basic conceptualizations of what we want to study. Our approach to, perceptions of, and interpretations of what we experience are filtered through a web of assumptions, expectations

---

[1]There are, however, some efforts to develop grounded theory; to move away from neo-positivism and incorporate some ideas of the constructed nature of social inquiry (Charmaz, 2000).

and vocabularies that will then guide entire projects and be crucial for the results we arrive at (e.g. Brown, 1977).

Somewhat more far-reaching critiques have been raised by *feminists* pointing at how male domination and masculine standards have influenced the dominant epistemology and methodology in social science (Jaggar, 1989). Male domination has produced a masculine social science built around ideals such as objectivity, neutrality, distance, control, rationality, and abstraction. Alternative ideals such as commitment, empathy, closeness, cooperation, intuition, and specificity have thereby been marginalized. Scientific rationality is thus expressing male domination, rather than superior reason. If one looks at the psychology of researchers and conflicts between different groups, the idea of the distanced and neutral scholar who is rationally oriented towards objective truth becomes peculiar (Bärmark, 1999; Popper, 1976). Researchers can often be very committed to their research and emotionally attached to theories and results. Critique and counter-evidence can then lead to defensiveness rather than a willingness to radically revise a position.

A related point of view has been expressed by *critical theorists* who would emphasize the political, interest- and value-laden nature of social enquiry (Alvesson & Deetz, 2000; Delanty, 2005; Kincheloe & McLaren, 1994). It is argued that knowledge development is grounded in human interests (Habermas, 1972). In social science, it is impossible to say anything of social significance without having some implications for the formation of society – social science is notoriously and inevitably political. Neither the researcher nor the other actors involved in influencing a research process and its outcome (research foundations, research leaders, editors and reviewers, the people studied and the mass media, and others who would guide them in how to think and how to express themselves) can exist in an ideological vacuum. It is seldom possible to identify and sort out the ideological from non-ideological elements when studying families, gender issues, the socialization of children, consumption, our care of elders, voting behavior, ethnicity, etc. The vocabulary is, for example, not neutral, even though commonly used language will often give the impression of being so. That human interests and cultural, gendered and political ideals can put their imprint on methodological ideals as well as on research practices and results makes it very difficult to see science as a pure activity – neutral and objective in relation to the reproduction or challenging of social ideologies, institutions and interests.

QUALITATIVE RESEARCH AND THEORY DEVELOPMENT

Even more profound are the views of *discursivists* and (other language-focused) constructivists which would deny science any privileged access to the objective truth about the social world outside language and language use (Potter & Wetherell, 1987; Steier, 1991). Language constructs rather than mirrors phenomena, making representation and thus empirical work a basically problematic enterprise, or so it is argued (Denzin & Lincoln, 2005; Gergen & Gergen, 1991). What (possibly) exists 'out there' (e.g. behaviors) or 'in there' (e.g. feelings or motives) is complex and ambiguous and can never simply be captured, but given the perspective, the vocabulary and the chosen interpretation, 'reality' can emerge in a particular way. Any claim of truth then says as much or more about the researcher's convictions and language use than about the object of study. Foucault (1980), one of the most influential social theorist (broadly defined) at present, claimed that social scientific knowledge was closely associated with power (the regulation of social reality through arrangements and ordering devices) and less with exploring or distorting truth than creating it.

To sum up, it is increasingly common to claim

> that there is no clear window into the inner life of an individual. Any gaze is always filtered through the lenses of language, gender, social class, race, and ethnicity. There are no objective observations, only observations socially situated in the worlds of the observer and the observed. (Denzin & Lincoln, 1994: 12)

The critique of positivism and neo-positivism is massive. However, this does not stop the majority of researchers from doing normal science more or less as if nothing has happened. Questionnaire researchers still assume that the X's put in small squares by respondents make it possible to determine what goes on in the social world. Qualitative researchers still present interview statements as if they were pathways to the interiors of those being interviewed and that observational data via codification and categories will mirror social practice, although it is broadly recognized – also amongst positivists – that data need to be interpreted to say anything. And that the process always involves the (selective and contestable) construction of data, as well as any use of it.

One problem with the critique of approaches having a strong faith in data is that it is perceived as categorical, provocative and destructive, and therefore is neglected. Another problem is that much of the critique addresses philosophical and epistemological issues, while the craft of doing research – for example fieldwork – has received much less attention. This is largely viewed – at least in most textbooks and also in research reports – as a technical matter, separated from theoretical and philosophical ideas about knowledge production, although some change is on the way here. Method (the action-related principles and ideas on how to produce and make sense of empirical material) still largely remains comparatively unaffected by all the work that has tremendous relevance for our understanding of methodological practices. The wealth of insights into problems of developing knowledge and the limitations to social science as a rational project need to be connected to research practices. Many researchers feel that all this philosophy of science and associated critique of traditional research are of limited relevance (e.g. Melia, 1997). We think the challenge is to try to incorporate parts of these into research practice. This rather heterogeneous but rapidly expanding critique of social research and its uncertain relevance for specific methods for doing fieldwork, interpreting and writing poses one context for this book.

The ambition then is to work with empirical material and to take it seriously without giving it a non-motivated robust status, as well as to treat it as if it offers a strong authority for forms of knowledge that are based on claims of being grounded in data and revealing reality. The ambition is also to put critical ideas about dataism into constructive use, where the possibilities – rather than the problems and impossibilities of empirical research – can be emphasized.

An Honest Account of How Empirical Material is Created and Processed

The aforementioned, more theoretically- and philosophically-based critique of empirical results as a solid building block in the accumulation of knowledge can be supplemented with some consideration of the practical problems of mirroring reality out there in research texts.

A major issue with the (limited) reliability of empirical studies concerns the many (more or less) coincidental and arbitrary ingredients required in the transportation of representations of whatever is supposed to be studied into the final research text. Given the many elements that matter, it is always highly uncertain what exactly the latter report will actually say about the former.

Let us illustrate this with the help of a short vignette. This is Dan's story of how he undertook his thesis:

I did my PhD thesis on the subject of the role of organizational culture in professional organizations – in my case, in the newsroom at an evening newspaper.

Methodologically, the study drew mainly from anthropological and ethnographic traditions. Consequently, I spent nine months (two or three days a week during the first six months and one day a week during the three subsequent months) participating in and observing everyday organizational activities.

I participated in and observed meetings, conversations between organizational members of different ranks and in different contexts and events occurring in a routine or non-routine fashion. I conversed with as many as possible on an informal basis, resulting in more than 100 interactions spanning from five minutes to several hours. I also interviewed 15 members with different roles and positions on a more formal basis, with each interview elapsing roughly one hour. The interviews and most meetings were taped and later transcribed. I also kept a diary where I made field notes on things that attracted my attention during the day.

As a result, I almost drowned in data. I had 250 pages of interview transcripts, roughly 700 pages of transcripts from meetings – I ended up with more than 100 hours of tapes from meetings, with each hour yielding about 20 pages of transcript and, in the end, I decided that it was simply not worth it to transcribe everything – and about 100 pages of field notes. Given my particular subject, some of the data seemed to be easy to organize – key symbols, dominant values, and so on. Other things were more difficult to get a grip on. Mundane meetings, routinized work procedures, non-descript office buildings and hallways didn't exactly provide a self-evident input to symbolic and cultural analysis. Most of my material, it occurred to me at the time, was redundant, irrelevant or unsurprising. Still, there were some discordant themes that nagged at me and that could not easily be dismissed as obvious, absurd or pointless. Why, for example, did there seem to be a qualitative difference between the two daily meetings between supervisors? Why was hierarchy both embraced and dismissed?

In the end, approximately 5 per cent of the data eventually showed up in the final thesis, mostly in the form of interview excerpts and excerpted transcripts from meetings. I do think that I am presenting at least a somewhat authoritative account of how an organization culture can co-ordinate activity in the newsroom. I am also the first to admit that another researcher may have chosen to put an emphasis on some other 5 per cent of the text – presumably reflecting what people said when interviewed by me or how I thought they acted and talked when observing them – or may have chosen to report another story, with the help of another subset of the empirical material, or may even have chosen to interpret my particular subset differently. There was, for example, some good stuff on how the media are key players in creating and constituting the contemporary culture that I could have done more with, but my academic affiliation (business administration) possibly made me less inclined to pursue this theme. If my advisor at the time – Mats – had had a smaller commitment to cultural analysis this would also likely have affected my choice of frame of reference.

This account of the problems inherent in condensing a great deal of empirical material into a manageable research report is quite typical for qualitative research. Apart from the inherent selective nature of research reports – one always has to reduce complex empirical material down to directly reporting interview citations and observations that will fill no more than 50 pages if publishing a monography, or no more than five to seven pages if publishing the research results in a journal – there are other concerns that will guide the creation of empirical material in the first place. There will be plenty of filtering elements elsewhere, emerging from the researcher, the research community and the society guiding the individual, as well as from those being studied. These concerns will include a researcher's personal and social background; his/her philosophical, theoretical and political commitments; the expectations and interests of the natives who are selectively reporting things (or perhaps modifying their behavior due to the researcher observing them); the interplay between the people being studied and the researcher; and the problem of ordering the material in a way that makes sense from a theoretical and paradigmatic perspective (Alvesson, 2002).

There are strong social pressures and convention-guided constraints that will put their imprint on the process and outcome. A researcher's work can often be seen as an effect of the various social forces at play and the pressure to show coherent and convincing results. A persuasive study mobilizes and prioritizes empirical material that clearly supports one case. Exercising caution in bringing forward observations, interview statements or artefacts that go in other directions or indicate that it is hard to say something decisive is a wise move here.

There is of course the norm that one should exhibit broad and representative empirical material, but one must also do so without giving too much space to material which is incoherent or ambiguous in relation to one's major idea and thesis. To be persuasive and to minimize the reader's doubts give the template for success.

This means that one can not just report a statistical representative of interview statements or observations without facing sanctions, as this would make its readers confused or unconvinced. Conventions for writing (like formatting, style, modes of persuasion and so on) must be adapted. Readers will often want convergence, support for a story, and clear and convincing patterns to be demonstrated. Even if one makes a case for ambiguity or contradiction for example, this should also be demonstrated in such a clear-cut way that the reader doesn't suspect some 'deeper' pattern behind any inconsistencies and confusions. (See Alvesson, 1993a, for a demonstration of how behind such claims about ambiguity the opposite element – a shared understanding – can be detected.) In practical terms, it is perhaps 5 per cent (or 1 per cent in an article) of all the available data presented that are, presumably in most cases, chosen, ordered and framed so that other people can be convinced that, 'Aha, here we have a valid empirical study'. As Alvesson et al. (2008) argue, it is in many cases the adaptation to and negotiations with the social and political context that are key driving elements behind a finished and published text.

This is not necessarily a bad thing and it is completely unavoidable. The legitimate researcher wants to craft a text that is well argued and convincing and claims a strong contribution, that is inextricably fused with selective reporting, interpretation and framing. Responses to advice from colleagues, editors, supervisors, reviewers; the anticipation of reader responses; commercial considerations about fashionable and hot topics, and so on – all of this will matter here and tend to contribute to an emphasis on coherence and the delivery of clear results. The final result – the text – will inevitably be the outcome of several complex processes, most of which simply couldn't be described in rational and objective ways. There are too many elements involved, which in turn may or may not have a strong impact on the study.

It is likely that another researcher, even if the purpose and object of research are the same, with another gender and political orientation, and having read (partly) other texts on method and theory as well as other empirical studies, would choose slightly different people to study, would use other categories and vocabularies, would encounter other colleagues, editors and reviewers – and so produce quite different research results. Our overall point is that this is the case *not only* because of the effect of the necessity of interpretations and constructions; the inability of language to mirror the world; the political context of social science; and the ambiguity and indecidability of major parts of social reality. It is *also* the case for very practical, down-to-earth reasons that can be associated with assembling research texts and getting them published and distributed to the wider world.

Our argumentation and overall point are illustrated in Figure 1.1. Conventionally, empirical studies would claim that the phenomenon studied (the cloud-like object to the left) is, at the end of the research project, authoritatively represented in the final text along with reliable indicators of that phenomenon (descriptions, interpretations, summarizing results). But one could argue that all the elements (a) to (g) in the figure follow partly different logics than just one of simply reflecting the characteristics of the object of study and that it is an open question as to which of these ingredients would have put the strongest imprint on the final text and its truth claims. Any of these may matter more than the 'objective' characteristics of the phenomenon presumed to have been studied. Taking this seriously suggests that we might consider empirical research in terms of its offering other virtues and contributions than mainly being about the accurate reporting of the phenomenon studied.

Empirical Material as a Critical Dialogue Partner

However, the focus in this book, as has already been mentioned, is not to demonstrate the problems with rationalistic approaches to research or to show what the research process 'really' looks like. Rather than engaging in a generic critique of the difficulties and relevance of doing empirical studies, we aim to put forward a constructive agenda. Thus we see empirical material as the outcome of various constructions – the effects of interpretations and a use of specific vocabularies – and as such it is fused together with theory rather than external to it. In this book we emphasize the potential of empirical material as a resource for developing theoretical ideas through the active mobilization and problematization of existing frameworks. In particular, we point to the ways in which empirical material can be mobilized to

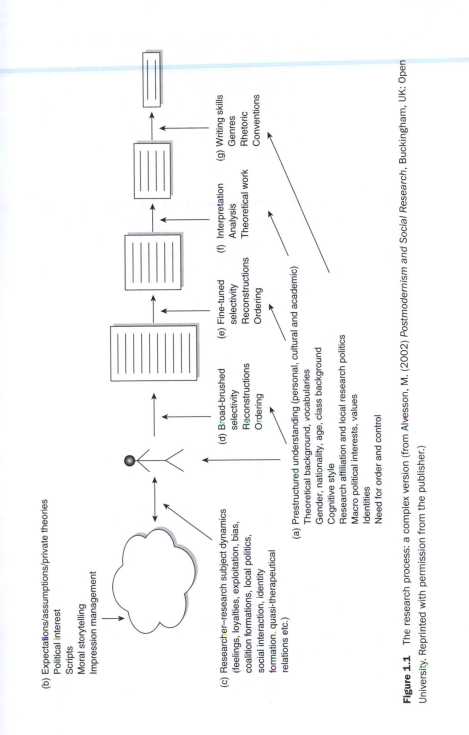

(b) Expectations/assumptions/private theories
Political interest
Scripts
Moral storytelling
Impression management

(c) Researcher–research subject dynamics
(feelings, loyalties, exploitation, bias,
coalition formations, local politics,
social interaction, identity
formation, quasi-therapeutical
relations etc.)

(a) Prestructured understanding (personal, cultural and academic)
Theoretical background, vocabularies
Gender, nationality, age, class background
Cognitive style
Research affiliation and local research politics
Macro political interests, values
Identities
Need for order and control

(d) Broad-brushed selectivity
Reconstructions
Ordering

(e) Fine-tuned selectivity
Reconstructions
Ordering

(f) Interpretation
Analysis
Theoretical work

(g) Writing skills
Genres
Rhetoric
Conventions

Figure 1.1 The research process: a complex version (from Alvesson, M. (2002) *Postmodernism and Social Research*, Buckingham, UK: Open University. Reprinted with permission from the publisher.)

facilitate and encourage critical reflection: to enhance our ability to challenge, refute, refine and illustrate theory.

This approach is informed by strong arguments against 'dataism' and a recognition of the constructed nature of empirical material and 'proofs' (Alvesson & Deetz, 2000; Astley, 1985; Shotter, 1993; Shotter & Gergen, 1994; Steier, 1991). It advocates a light or moderate version of constructionism – assuming that something is going on out there and that there may be better or worse ways of addressing things. We propose a relaxation of the emphasis on robust 'data' for the benefit of our consideration of empirical material as a strong but also flexible input for theoretical reasoning (c.f. Sutton & Staw, 1995). From a post-empiricist standpoint, this orientation towards empirical findings offers a viable way forward, especially for those who are interested in what may be encountered in empirical work and who would recognize that all empirical material is constructed, being irredeemably fused with theory and interpretation. This orientation goes against the conventional neo-positivistic criteria favored by advocates of objectivistic-dataistic qualitative research (a type of grounded theory; see Alvesson & Sköldberg, 2009; Denzin, 1994). However, it does not reject the possibility that some interpretations or constructions may be more empirically supported and qualified than others.

In conventional terms, we shall focus on the discovery (or even better the creation) of theory, rather than its justification. Although we do find novel approaches towards the refinement and justification of theory valuable, we aim for more creative ways of theorizing. Like many others, we would claim that data (or our preferred term 'empirical material') are simply not capable of showing the right route to theory or screening good ideas from the bad. Rather, empirical material is an artifact of interpretations and the use of specific vocabularies. As will be repeated a few times in this book, data are inextricably fused with theory. Acknowledging this fusion – which is broadly accepted in the philosophy of science (Denzin & Lincoln, 2000; Gergen, 1978; Kuhn, 1970; Rorty, 1979; Wittgenstein, 1953) – has major consequences for how we should consider the theory–empirical material relationship. Empirical material should be opened up rather than viewed as a source of constraint and discipline in research work.

As we see it, the interplay between theory and empirical material is more about seeing the latter as a source of inspiration and as a *partner for critical dialogue*. Empirical material is then *not viewed as a*

QUALITATIVE RESEARCH AND THEORY DEVELOPMENT

guide to or as the ultimate validator for knowledge claims. The latter seems to be the preferred root metaphor in method books and in reported empirical studies, but as we outlined above it relies on problematic assumptions. Although fieldwork in social science is typically performed among speaking objects (subjects) one must remember that social reality never speaks for itself. It always speaks through a language that is familiar to and favoured by the speaker; a matter further complicated by the fact that in social science it is not only the subject but also the researcher who will act as mediators of the social world. We must recognize our pre-understanding as researchers (and as subjects targeted for study as well) and our active involvement in construction processes. This opens up the way for more interesting and reflexive constructions that can allow empirical materials to speak back to pre-understandings and theoretical ideas. To engage with empirical material as a critical dialogue partner is thus difficult and challenging. It clearly moves beyond a grounded theory-like codification and the discovery of categories. The very outlook on knowledge creation is fundamentally different.

A key element here is the role of empirical material in inspiring the *problematization* of theoretical ideas and vocabularies. To problematize means to challenge the value of a theory as well as to explore its weaknesses and problems in relation to the phenomena it is supposed to explicate. It also means to generally open this up and to point out the need and possible directions for rethinking and developing it. We consequently attempt to develop a methodology for theory development through encounters between theoretical assumptions and empirical impressions that involve breakdowns. It is the unanticipated and the unexpected – the things that puzzle researchers – that are of particular interest in such encounters. In this sense, our approach attempts to take systematic advantage of what Robert Merton labels serendipity: 'the art of being curious at the opportune but unexpected moment' (Merton & Barber, 2004: 210). Accordingly, theory development is stimulated and facilitated through a selective interest in what does *not* work in an existing theory, in the sense of encouraging interpretations that will allow a productive and non-commonsensical understanding of an ambiguous social reality.

The empirical material, when carefully constructed, thus forms a strong impetus for rethinking the conventional wisdom. However, the ideal is *not*, as in neo-positivist work, to aim for an 'intimate interaction with actual evidence' that 'produces theory which closely mirrors

15

reality' (Eisenhardt, 1989: 547).[2] The empirical material may be mobilized as a critical dialogue partner – not as a judge or a mirror – which problematizes a significant form of understanding, thus encouraging problematization and theoretical insights (c.f. Ragin, 1987; ch. 9). The dialogue metaphor is not uncommon in contemporary qualitative research. Emphasizing the critical aspect of theory as well as data construction, and therefore involving a careful consideration of alternative representations, frames the enterprise somewhat differently to that found in established views. We think it is important to draw attention to the construction of friction as a potentially productive force rather than to any harmony in the interplay between theory, researcher subjectivity and empirical material.

Rather than displaying a positive process of mutual support, where theory guides empirical work, data modify theory, etc., the theory-impregnated nature of empirical material is emphasized and the value of developing friction and conflict between various possibilities in constructing data is highlighted.

Research as the Creation of Mystery

We have been inspired here by the Swedish sociologist Johan Asplund's stimulating (1970) idea of social science as involving two elements: the discovery or creation of a breakdown in understanding in theoretical interest (the construction of a mystery) and the recovery of this understanding (the resolution of the mystery).[3] Asplund views writing (good) social science as similar to writing a (good) detective

---

[2]Neo-positivism (or post-positivism) assumes the existence of a reality that can be apprehended accurately but also imperfectly and probabilistically, where the observer and the observed can be separated, and the data and theory can be treated as separable, although the theory-ladenness of data is acknowledged. The aim is to produce generalizable results (Lincoln & Guba, 2000). Most contemporary quantitative social research and qualitative research like grounded theory (although there are different versions of the latter; see Charmaz, 2000) appear to be based on neo-positivist assumptions.

[3]Asplund (1970) develops two metaphors for creating novel understanding of social reality: the riddle and the crime mystery. In this chapter we use a generalized version of the mystery metaphor as a device for developing theory.

story. You create a mystery and then you solve it. In a sense, our project also shows an affinity with Poole and Van de Ven's (1989) suggestion of viewing paradoxes as resources for theorizing, and with Abbott's stimulating (2004) account of heuristics as a method for discovery. However, in contrast to Asplund's and Poole and Van de Ven's strong focus on armchair theorizing, and Abbott's somewhat misguided attempt to be exhaustive, we would pay particular attention here to the interplay between theory and empirical material, thus focusing on how the inconsistencies and breakdowns derived from empirical observation, rather than from (pure) theoretical speculation, may help us to develop theory.

Put succinctly, we aim to take the mystery creation and solving approach to the field and develop it in the context of empirical research, showing how impressions of social reality can be a major source for developing new and challenging insights and, subsequently, for developing theory. Chiefly, our goal is to explore how empirical material can be used to develop theory that is interesting rather than obvious, irrelevant or absurd (Davis, 1971). A key element here is challenging the assumptions within the particular field one wishes to contribute to. This can of course be done through problematizing an existing theory as well as studies in a field via critical scrutiny, combined with efforts to produce alternative ideas (Alvesson & Sandberg, 2011), but the objective for this book is to explore how empirical inquiry can be used to challenge assumptions.

It is, of course, not just a question of 'pure' empirical inquiry, as this view of research casts its shadow on the research questions asked, our reading of literature, fieldwork design, tactics, interpretations during and after fieldwork, reinterpretations and writing up research texts. All these elements are important as well as related, and a researcher – having adopted a mystery-view – will go back and forth between different parts of the research process in, at best, creatively stimulating ways. (However, in this book we focus on empirical studies. We shall try not to do this narrowly or strictly, as we of course will touch upon other related issues as well.)

Theorization may be understood as disciplined imagination (Mills, 1959; Weick, 1989). Empirical material can facilitate theorization because it provides resources for both imagination and discipline. And although empirical material never exists outside perspectives and interpretative repertoires, it nevertheless creates a relative boundary for imagination. Some constructions make more sense than others. Many appear far-fetched or pointless. This is partly a matter of experience of empirical accuracy. Empirical material anchors the process of theorization in specific claims about the object under study, thus prohibiting arbitrary ideas from being put into play. An important element here is to realize that empirical material may feed into rethinking the obvious. This is mainly provided by experiences indicating that the assumptions of conventional wisdom – a tradition, a school of thought, or a framework of theories – are problematic, and where prevailing understandings break down. Breakdowns may appear problematic initially, but they also create spaces where imagination can be put to work.

Consider, for example, Weick's (1993) interpretation of the Mann Gulch disaster – an event that killed 13 firefighters in an explosive forest fire. The central breakdown in this came when a well-trained group of smoke-jumpers ceased to operate as a professional unit and began to disintegrate and panic with catastrophic results. Weick maintained that the main rationale for the disintegration of the organization could be traced to a collapse in sense-making. His argument was that as long as the fire behaved as the team had expected the unit would have operated normally, but when it had unexpectedly turned into an explosive firestorm, a change that was only picked up by the group leader, there was a catastrophic loss of meaning. The other group members had then failed to grasp the reason for the leader's abrupt change of procedure – which included lighting a fire in front of the crew and thus creating a fire escape, all the while urging them to drop their tools and jump into the ash-filled area. This led to a collapse in understanding, which then led to a sudden disintegration of the organization and thus to panic, which caused the 13 fatalities (the group leader survived). Weick resolved the 'mystery' by pointing out that, contrary to conventional wisdom, panic results from organization disintegration rather than the other way around, and that the organization disintegration was the result of getting stuck in an interpretation of events that suddenly ceased to be justified, thus suggesting that meaning is primary to structure.

Another example here is provided by Ashcraft's (2000) paper on the bureaucratization of personal relationships in a feminist organization. Her study was situated in a shelter for victims of domestic violence, which explicitly embraced diversity, feminist leadership and countercultural practices such as 'ethical communication'. Briefly, ethical communication could be viewed as an attempt to create undistorted communication. Members were expected to express themselves authentically and members expected to have sufficient space to articulate themselves. This was taken very seriously at the shelter and was viewed as the centerpiece for enabling empowerment and realizing the feminist ethos. Bureaucracy was viewed with suspicion – a suspicion that Ashcraft noted was shared by most of the literature on feminist organizing. Accordingly, one would have expected the shelter to have been a lively place where members and volunteers were unafraid to express themselves and to engage freely in conversation, and where emotions and feelings were vividly on display. Largely, this was also what Ashcraft found, with one highly notable exception. As it happened, concerns had mounted between members on the appropriateness of certain types of relationships at work. In particular, romantic and sexual relationships between affiliates had begun to be constructed as highly problematic, and this had also extended to friendships. The solution to this perceived problem was to institute a highly specific policy on the type of relationships that was allowed between affiliates, a policy that was also largely effectively policed. In effect, the policy prescribed that relationships between affiliates had to be professional and detached, at least in terms of romance, sexuality, and friendship.

How is it possible that an explicitly feminist organization with institutionalized feminist practices could end up with policies that were at odds with a feminist ethos, and could actually embrace the bureaucratic principles that feminism explicitly rejects? The resolution to this mystery could mostly be found, Ashcraft argued, in the intense wariness that existed around the notion of power at the shelter. All of the problems that are supposed to emerge from romantic, sexual and friendship relationships coalesce around notions of the abuse of power. As Ashcraft noted, it was not surprising that this argument had clout in an environment that explicitly fought violence and abuse, although here it took on a neurotic, if not a power-phobic, form.

Exploiting breakdowns is, of course, not new to social science. In particular, in ethnographic work and especially in anthropology the initial difference between the traditions involved (the researcher's and the topic of study) produces breakdowns in understanding: 'A breakdown is a lack of fit between one's encounter with a tradition and the schema-guided expectations by which one organizes experience' (Agar, 1986: 21). The researcher resolves this problem by trying to understand the cultural elements that are causing the breakdown, and then by adjusting the research schema. Breakdowns will continue to appear until the researcher sufficiently understands the studied culture. This means that ethnography can be described 'as a process of coherently resolving breakdowns' (Agar, 1986: 39).

In this sense, ethnography has an in-built propensity towards the type of theory development we outline in this chapter. So this is the case at least if ethnographic inquiry is informed by theoretical ambitions – sometimes the target of ethnography will be thick description, which will fall short of a theoretical ambition.

However, ethnography is far from being the only method that is capable of taking advantage of breakdowns for developing new theoretical ideas. In any kind of study there is always the potential for something that will speak out sufficiently firmly against the assumptions and reasoning that the researcher holds and is engaged in. An example of quantitative studies producing a breakdown is Lincoln and Kalleberg's (1985) piece on job satisfaction and organizational commitment among US and Japanese workers. The result showed higher scores for the former which certainly was surprising, as the general view during this time, when Japanese companies were very successful, was that their workforce had a much stronger work ethic than their US competitors did. The 'mystery' here can possibly be solved by seeing questionnaire responses less as objective measurements of objective phenomena and more as clues to the cultural norms for expressions and following language rules (Alvesson & Deetz, 2000). The questionnaire is perhaps not so much an instrument for accessing people's attitudes than for judging how they tend to follow norms and conventions in expressing themselves. Another example is that of the classical Hawthorne studies, focusing on job performances, human relations and norms of performance among factory workers in the 1920s and 1930s. This research started with experiments on how light could affect performance. The hypothesis was that better light would increase productivity and at the beginning this was indeed confirmed. Increased light increased worker productivity. But this same productivity also continued to rise when the light's strength was decreased. This came as a great surprise to the researchers, who had to rethink their original hypothesis. This led to open-ended ethnographic research that radically explored new ideas about the dynamics of social interactions in the workplace and group norms – a shift that had clearly been encouraged by the empirical material that had challenged the initial research framework (c.f. Schwartzman, 1993).

Our objective in this book is to suggest an approach to theory development that uses theory and imagination to critically open up alternative ways of framing empirical material. Here we are following a large amount of work in methodology, including significant contributions by

Asplund (1970), Abbott (2004), Peirce (1978), Mills (1959), Garfinkel (1967), Gergen (1978), Davis (1971), Becker (1996), Weick (1989) and many others in the philosophy of science and interpretive social science. Critical reflection, theory-driven disclosure, and the specific procedure of working with breakdowns and mysteries combine to create an overall methodology. This systematizes attempts to explore new terrain and develop novel ideas, thus potentially overcoming the inherent conservatism in well-established frameworks. We focus on exploring a maximalist version of breakdown-induced theory development. However, we also address broader strategies for taking advantage of breakdowns for theory development. Our ambition is not to try to colonize empirical research through a specific design, but to provide some overall guidelines and concepts which can be potentially useful for novel theorizing.

Outline of the Book

Apart from this chapter, in which we have outlined our overall approach, the book consists of seven chapters including this one.

The following chapter deals with constructionist ideas and discusses the role of language and vocabulary, emphasizing the power of a specific research language to (seemingly) control and order the world. Traditional views of language as something that the researcher controls and through which empirical reality is authoritatively captured are critically addressed. How language constitutes the object of study and results also demands consideration. The need to be reflective and to realize vocabularies other than the preferred one – or the culturally dominating vocabulary – are also discussed.

Chapter 3 looks in detail at the norm of exploring patterns in social science. Although identifying patterns is an important exercise in research, it is less helpful for the kind of research we are discussing in this book. Therefore we suggest that theory is likely to emerge through the challenging of established patterns rather than through attempts to put the bits of the jigsaw back together. We introduce five principles – (de-)fragmentation, defamiliarization, problematization, scholarship (broad education or, to use a German term, *bildung* [building]) and reflexive critique – by which to challenge established frames of understanding.

Chapter 4 introduces a five-step guideline, or heuristic (Abbott, 2004), for identifying and constructing mysteries that are suitable for

THE USE OF EMPIRICAL MATERIAL FOR THEORY DEVELOPMENT

theory development: i) familiarization; ii) enacting a breakdown; iii) elevating a breakdown into a mystery; iv) solving that mystery; and v) developing a resolution. The chapter also discusses some more general ideas on breakdowns and mysteries and how these are cultivated.

Chapter 5 attempts to illustrate the principles outlined in Chapter 3 and the guidelines suggested in Chapter 4 with three empirical cases. These consist of materials on gender structure in the advertising industry; patterns of conversation and identification in a meeting at an evening edition newspaper; and human resource management practices at a management-consulting firm.

Chapter 6 makes a link between our overall methodological framework and specific forms of method/fieldwork. On the whole, the framework can be used irrespective of the type of qualitative or quantitative method, but in qualitative studies one can sometimes mobilize those studied in line with the framework and with a process element that makes mystery creation but in particular, mystery solving easier. We illustrate this with interview research and suggest some ideas on how to address interviewees and conduct interviews, thereby increasing the chances of a productive use of the mystery methodology.

Chapter 7 summarizes our efforts. This is partly done through pointing at our proposed set of metaphors for understanding research and its components, e.g. the view of the nature and role of data/empirical material. The chapter also points to less ambitious ways of applying the ideas brought forward in the book. We here distinguish between breakdown-focused, breakdown-sensitive and breakdown-considering approaches, depending on the level of ambition present when searching for and working with mysteries.

2

THE ROLE OF CONSTRUCTIONS AND LANGUAGE IN EMPIRICAL RESEARCH

As mentioned in the previous chapter, social science is typically assumed to advance through the generation of new knowledge, either by the accumulation of verified (or corroborated) hypotheses or by the discovery of theory by sifting through mountains of data. However, both the accumulation view – using theory to find knowledge gaps – and the grounded theory 'discovery' view are problematic.

A key ingredient in most research, but most clearly the case in the accumulation view, is to review the literature and then identify a white spot on the knowledge map (Locke & Golden-Biddle, 1997; Sandberg & Alvesson, 2011). The overall logic here is one of 'map-and-fill-the-gap'. These are strongly dominating hypothesis-testing studies that typically heavily emphasize the accumulation of knowledge. Theory guides hypothesizing and is corrected by the outcome of the tested hypotheses. If research has been carried out and evidence has been gathered and found to be conclusive, then a robust chunk of knowledge has been established and progress can be made. New white spots on the knowledge map may then have been identified and such gaps must be filled with new studies. Gap-spotting, gap-filling, and the accumulation of knowledge become the key logic of research.

So-called discovery approaches like grounded theory are different in the sense that existing studies do not represent a major point of departure. They typically privilege data and give an impression of rationality through emphasizing procedures, rules, and a clear route from empirical reality via data to theory (Eisenhardt, 1989; Glaser & Strauss, 1967; Strauss & Corbin, 1994). Diligent work with 'data processing' is central here. The critique of this approach has emphasized an over-reliance on pure 'data' and a neglect of the constructed nature of empirical material, the centrality of theory, language and the researcher in producing representations and empirical results (Alvesson & Sköldberg, 2009; Charmaz, 2000; Lincoln & Guba, 2000). In addition, the strict focus on the codification and processing of data leads to a time-consuming, cautious, and constrained approach that hampers theory-development.

Of course, gap-filling studies and GT 'discovery' work have their role to play. Identifying blind spots or unsolved issues through careful literature reviews is the obvious way taken by positivist empirical research. Indeed qualitative researchers will often do something similar. The idea is that earlier studies will have generally established firm knowledge, but there will still be areas left to study or controversies and uncertainties about knowledge if and when researchers have accumulated opposite or inconclusive results. These two logics – as major elements in a large amount of studies – assume a robustness to earlier studies and data, at least if these have been carried out according to the proper prescription for doing good research. Both assume that empirically verified knowledge is the cornerstone of knowledge development, encircling data as the major fundament for research.

The discovery metaphor is significant here. Knowledge and theory are about discovering something 'out there'. Even if this 'out there' covers experiences, meanings or emotions, it can still be assumed to be existing 'objectively' and can be found; it does not prevent the researcher from claiming to report 'findings'. Implicitly the geographer-explorer of past times is the model here. We identify research problems with the knowledge gap through mapping earlier research and locating the white spots, or by seeing where the terrain has not been scrutinized and mapped in a sufficiently correct and precise way – resulting in controversies between researchers who have produced divergent results. For grounded theorists we can only discover something through a detailed and careful study of the data – the landscape. This mapping metaphor is to some extent in line with practitioner interests. For practitioner-oriented researchers, interested in an issue that represents a basic concern in a local context and inspires inductive and 'practice-near' work, grounded theory work that tries to develop a locally relevant theory is a crucial project.

Both of the map-the-gap and the discovery views described above can be contrasted with a constructionist approach.[1] In the latter we

---

[1]The term 'construction' has its drawbacks, as it misleadingly indicates something robust and stable, but as it is established and indicates the active and innovative element in producing versions of reality we shall accept it and use it here.

QUALITATIVE RESEARCH AND THEORY DEVELOPMENT

construct rather than collect data. We don't discover knowledge or theory, and we do not believe that data can be used as reliable informants for what is true or false. Taking the construction metaphor seriously means that the landscape and its mapping will always become uncertain, precarious, and metaphorical. We cannot build theory on a solid foundation, as what is supposed to be the latter is, in social science, typically neither solid nor a foundation. Established and accumulated knowledge is not necessarily authoritative and unproblematic enough that we can proceed from it and focus on what remains to be explored. Even if there is a high level of consensus and an established and received truth amongst a number of researchers, there may still be good reasons to look seriously and skeptically at the assumptions and construction processes involved in the production and reproduction of this truth. With accumulated knowledge we can often also find an accumulation of problematic assumptions and a range of problems regarding, say, ontology, epistemology, and language use.

Although it has become commonplace to regard social research as being about constructions, the meaning and implication of this are viewed very differently (Barlebo Wennerberg, 2001; Knorr Cetina, 1994). Sometimes it will take the form that von Glasersfeld (1991) refers to as 'trivial constructions', i.e. the people under study are constructing their reality, which is something that researchers can investigate 'objectively'. Constructions need to be taken seriously in a variety of respects – not only how natives construct, but also how researchers construct their constructions. The latter is of major concern in this book: how a researcher construction can create a mystery as a platform for theory development via that mystery's solution.

In this chapter we shall address some constructionist ideas on knowledge development and a key element within these: how we may understand language. The overall intention here is to provide various arguments for an approach to empirical work where the ambiguity and open nature of data must be recognized and be seen as something not to be denied or marginalized, but as a possibility for doing more interesting and creative work, and with a better chance to develop new and challenging theory than simply characterizing 'dataistic' work.

Construction rather than Verification

A key quality of data is normally understood to be the capacity to correct ideas and statements about reality. This correction capacity is central not only in verification attempts, but also in inductive work like grounded theory and phenomenology that relies on data. As mentioned in Chapter 1, much of the recent developments in social theory, philosophy of science and methodology have tended to downplay the role of empirical material as a validator of 'objective reality' (Alvesson & Sköldberg, 2009; Denzin & Lincoln, 2000; Rorty, 1979; Rosenau, 1992). Three arguments are important here:

- First, as stated above, there are good reasons to follow the trend away from dataism/empiricism and towards a realization that data are fused with theory and interpretation in contemporary social science and philosophy of science. This means that there is a problem in using data as something that is clearly capable of saying yes or no to various claims. This is not to deny that sometimes empirical results can give indications as to whether an idea is true or not, but most of the non-simple research problems that are of broad intellectual interest tend to be more complicated and less than well-suited for hypothesis-testing.
- Secondly, irrespective of the verification possibilities for empirical material, the degree to which theories are supported or not by data does not seem to influence how people value theory. Empirical verification is not insignificant, but on the whole appears to have a rather limited relevance for assessing the value of a theoretical contribution:

> Theories gain favor because of their conceptual appeal, their logical structure, or their psychological plausibility. Internal coherence, parsimony, formal elegance, and so on prevail over empirical accuracy in determining a theory's impact. (Astley, 1985: 503)

This may be an outcome of the boundedness of human rationality: we may like things that are fun and fashionable for example, rather than what seems to be well supported. This can be viewed as a source of worry rather than as a reason to celebrate virtues other than empirical support for a theory. As scholars are not in the entertainment business some concerns against the celebration of those ideas that appear fun, creative and novel are bound to arise.[2] But this may also say something about what we find valuable in terms of adding to our knowledge and thinking. And here we mean that not just logic, but also imagination, excitement, aesthetics and other 'non-rational' elements are vital. Virtues like being interesting and challenging matter more than the exact degree of support. It is probably also the

---

[2] One may suspect that some of the success of the more drastic versions of postmodernism in the late eighties and early nineties may be related to the comparatively high entertainment value of this approach, celebrating irony and playfulness.

case that the theories which many people find interesting are not so easy to test. Psychoanalysis, evolution, and Foucauldian ideas on power/knowledge would be obvious examples of these.

- Thirdly, even if empirical verification were indeed possible, this would only be helpful to researchers if one assumes that we are on the brink of an almost perfect understanding of the social world. It would make sense to concentrate on a verification if, and only if, 'mankind is at the edge of an intellectual mastery of [the social world], approaching a capability to lay out a structured set of propositions describing it with scientific precision' (Lindblom, 1987: 514, in Weick, 1989: 524). However, as we all know, the social world is far from being perfectly understood. Moreover, it contains abrupt, unexpected, and far-reaching change processes – some of them fuelled by social science itself – that, among other things, will tend to render many empirical findings obsolete or at least of questionable relevance over time. As the social world can be produced in different ways, we need also consider alternative practices that for some reason or another were not chosen (Kreiner & Mouritsen, 2005). In this social world, our social world, it thus makes sense to put less emphasis on verification and validation, and to push another agenda forward:

> If validation is not a criterion for retaining conjectures, this means at least two things. First, the criteria used in place of validation must be explored carefully since the theorist, not the environment, now controls the survival of conjectures. Second, the contribution of social science does not lie in validated knowledge, but rather in the suggestion of relationships and connections that had not previously been suspected, relationships that change actions and perspectives. (Weick, 1989: 524)

For advocates of hypothesis-testing these three arguments against placing verification as the key concern for science may sound alarming. But few would argue for a complete rejection of the notion of letting empirical material kick back against ideas. The issue is more one of acknowledging the limits of verification and upgrading other virtues. We want theories that make us able to 'see' new issues and themes, ask new questions, challenge the established wisdom, open up alternative lines of thinking, inform careful and sometimes even bold interpretations, and so on. Still, it makes sense to see plausibility – rather than validity – as one important criterion for a good theory (Weick, 1989).

Giving empirical verification a less prominent place is well motivated if we consider all the difficulties within such an enterprise. Empirical evidence is constructed within particular paradigmatic and linguistic conventions and is typically less robust when approached from any other angle. While we should not reduce the value of empirical material as an important partner in any enterprise trying to develop knowledge, we should also not necessarily give it the role of ultimate validator, capable of saying yes (verification) or no (falsification) in response to ideas. Most interesting (complex) ideas cannot be easily 'checked' against data and empirical measures are always contestable.

> Ideas about empirical evidence, objectivity, reason, truth, coherence, validity, measurement, and fact no longer provide great comfort or direction. If such concepts are relative, not absolute, they are always contestable in whatever form they appear – although this is not to say that such concepts are thereby rendered irrelevant or unthinkable. (Van Maanen, 1995: 15)

One can also add that, as most phenomena worth investigating are complex, dynamic and difficult to observe, rigorous studies will have their limits and the researcher will have to depend on assumptions, maps, and metaphors (Alvesson and Sköldberg, 2009; Morgan, 1980; Weick, 1989). We are all the time engaged in making constructions of phenomena, which in themselves are constructions of actors and groups, anchored in and reproducing cultures and institutions. As discussed at length in the previous chapter, this is not to imply that empirical work is not valuable. The problems inherent with conventional claims of verification and falsification should not prevent researchers from carrying out ethnographic and other types of fieldwork with the ambition of producing and presenting rich studies in which empirical work and its outcomes are taken seriously. But here researchers, and – indirectly – the research community they bring in to guide the work, should be activated and confronted with the empirical material produced.

Viewing data as constructions – created through interactions between the researcher and the group under study, with a strong element of researcher invention – motivates a thinking-through of which metaphors should be used for the research project. Since the metaphor 'data collection' tends to be understood far too literally and is thus potentially misleading, we prefer, as noted above, 'empirical material' as a better representation of what is conventionally understood as data. The metaphorical quality of 'material' indicates that we, as researchers, must actively do something with it – it is more like clay than stone, if one finds it necessary to draw a parallel with the physical world. With this in mind we will use these terms interchangeably: data should be read as ambiguous empirical material standing indirectly and frequently loosely for social reality 'out there'. A key assumption behind this is that '[i]n the social sciences there is only interpretation. Nothing speaks for itself' (Denzin, 1994: 500). We can't avoid creating constructions for all the possible perceptions and indicators of how to make sense of social phenomena empirically. It is a challenge – and also a possibility – to take these constructions seriously.

Language Perspectivating rather than Mirroring Social Phenomena

A key aspect of constructions is language. Phenomena can be constructed in different ways and the vocabulary that is used in perception, description, analysis and writing in research will determine the results. Sensitivity to language is vital in order to make construction work productive and thoughtful. Most conventional research assumes that language operates as a kind of medium – albeit an imperfect one due to noise, distortion and ambiguity – which ideally mirrors the world 'out there'.

However, the linguistic turn in social science has attacked this language-as-mirror perspective (Alvesson & Kärreman, 2000; Potter & Wetherell, 1987; c.f. Rorty, 1979) by pointing out that all observation and data is theory-laden and embedded in language. Language use, in any social context, is active, processual, and outcome-oriented. It is used to persuade, enjoy, engage, discipline, criticize, express feelings, clarify, unite, perform identity work, and so on. Other authors emphasize how language and understanding are fused with, and indeed rely on, metaphors. Language – as a vital part not only of our cognitions, but also of our basic way of relating to the world – is metaphorical (Brown, 1977; Morgan, 1980; 1983). We live by metaphors (Lakoff & Johnson, 1980). Language is also context-dependent. One statement may have various meanings. For instance, saying 'the time is nine o' clock' may infer blame ('you are late'), or signal the start of a meeting, or be a response to a question, a preparation for a coordination of action through a synchronization of time, an encouragement to consider how time should be used; it all depends on the situation.

The production of scientific discourse – such as texts on social behavior – is as functional and constructive in its character as other, less sacrosanct, types of discourse. Texts are oriented towards creating effects rather than mirroring a phenomenon in social reality. Contrary to popular opinion, research texts are not – and cannot be – objective and clinical reports on 'how the facts are'. Rather, they engage in the persuasive construction of 'facts' through powerful modes of construction, where use of a clinically objective researcher's voice is one particularly powerful – although not necessarily defendable – mode (Van Maanen, 1995; Watson, 1994).

In a sense the problems of using language to map an external world are obvious and ought to be broadly recognized. The relationship between words like love, attitudes, higher education, family, racism, equal opportunity, knowledge, healthcare, profession, and quality, and whatever other phenomena are out there, tends to be ambiguous and loose. It is even possible that 'everybody' in academia knows that language is not a simple medium for the transport of meaning. At the very least 'everybody' knows that language is complicated. And yet working and writing *as if* the idea or ideal is that language may well be a medium for the transport of meaning does seem to be common in social science. Some researchers will insist on the use of literal language. They wish to avoid metaphors or other modes of expression that seem to deviate from the ideal of making possible a correspondence between research language and empirical reality. Or, less extreme, they want to limit the use of metaphors and other tropes to the initial, generative phase of research (c.f. Pinder & Bourgeois, 1982; Tsoukas, 1991).

In most empirical research, the research design and the research text will be developed and written as if the language is being strictly controlled by the researcher, a simple tool through which s/he will mirror the world. This is most obvious in questionnaire studies, as it presupposes that respondents will understand the formulated questions exactly or at least roughly as intended. We, the authors of this book, are presumably not the only ones often feeling lost when asked to respond to a questionnaire. Questions can very often be interpreted in various ways, making quite different responses equally possible. And giving a poor, biased, and partly misleading representation or hint of whatever phenomena the questionnaire items are supposed to reflect is probably common. Here the research practice often simply suppresses the basic problem of using language as a simple medium for accessing reality through collected data.

The vast majority of qualitative work, however, will follow a similar logic of aiming to control meaning through language. The difference typically will be that qualitative research will take a greater interest in the level of meaning and will also seek to provide space for research subjects to express their opinions via their own words. In being able to choose the words themselves, these research subjects are presumed to communicate their feelings, thoughts, values, experiences and observations in such a way that this will render their 'inner worlds' accessible to the researcher. Interview statements, for example, are seen as reflections of these 'inner worlds'. Alternatively, statements are viewed as mirroring or at least in most cases as saying something reliable about external phenomena (structures, practices). The assumption – and the claim in research reports – is that language and language use will represent something other than themselves.

The researcher, following this mirror logic, collects data and consequently builds a case, with the potential exclusion of material that is considered irrelevant or low in quality. In qualitative research the researcher presents selected portions of the research in order to prove the case. In quantitative studies statistical data and correlations are regularly proffered as if these were creating a window by which to view conditions outside of the questionnaire-filling situation. Given this encompasses methodologically competent research practice, the language use of informants (questionnaire respondents) is then seen as a reliable indicator of the issues in which the researcher is interested.

It is easy, based on a more sophisticated view of language, to simply reject this, however we think that this would overstate the case against language as mirror. It is, as we see it, also worthwhile to draw attention to the *relative* capacity of language to (equivocally) convey insights, experiences and factual information, as well as to recognize the *pragmatic* value of emphasizing its capacity to clarify phenomena. Criticism of a naive view of representation does not motivate a categorical rejection of the communicative powers of language – a move that can easily be read as destructive. As Rorty, in a critique of Lyotard (1984), puts it: 'For language no more has a nature than humanity does; both have only a history. There is as much unity or transparency of language as there is willingness to converse rather than fight' (1992: 66).

We think it is reasonable to emphasize the *partial* ability of language to convey something beyond itself. This means recognizing the potential capacity in accounts (however imperfect, mediated, and partial) to indicate realities beyond the situational and functional aspects of language use. It also means remaining reflective and skeptical, but not categorical, about the discursive level in research. It is, thus, essential to consider the extent to which various utterances can appropriately be treated simply as utterances, and how far these can be used as a starting-point for more extensive, speculative interpretations of other conditions, e.g. of behaviors, practices, and structures, and events, or of ideas, values, or experiences.

31

Instead of treating the problem of representation as an absolute, categorically assuming that we cannot represent anything whatsoever (except, perhaps, texts), *we may see the problem of representation as relative and contingent.* There are many situations and phenomena where representation does not seem to be very problematic and where researchers may be wise in treating the relationship between a signifier, or a combination of signifiers, as saying something about social reality. The statement that this text was originally written with some sort of writing device (in our case, Macintosh word processors) is probably acceptable to most people irrespective of their cultural or theoretical background and the point in emphasizing the undecidabilities of the signifier Macintosh word processor seems to be limited in most situations where people use it. This is probably also acceptable to those rejecting a correspondence view of language. The same would go for statements such as the use of condoms may protect people against AIDS or sexually transmitted diseases; the Nazis murdered millions of Jews, Romanies and other people they viewed as undesirable; penicillin is more effective than prayer for curing a number of diseases; and the Old Testament is not an instruction manual for the best way to to play bridge.

The representational capacity of language may never be entirely unproblematic, but the significance of this problem can vary, depending on the issues at hand. Language may not be capable of representing reality *in toto*, but it does indeed seem capable of providing the means to sometimes communicate instructively in and on various realities. This does not imply that we would basically adopt a view of language as capable of representing reality as if words could mirror nature. Vocabularies simply don't mirror the world – they produce and conceal as much as they reveal. The language used in a study to a large extent will determine the results. It is important to use language as a way to mobilize alternative vocabularies and to open up the way for alternative constructions, and not merely as a tool for passive reflection or the mirroring of phenomena.

Seeing language as something that perspectivizes is fruitful, as different language uses will lead to different perspectives/vocabularies being invoked then being various aspects then being rendered for further consideration. Language as a perspectivator is, in our view, a more productive way of understanding the relationship between language and social reality, rather than viewing it as a mirror of reality or as a world of its own, totally uncoupled from extra-discursive reality. Social reality is not denied, marginalized, seen as a pure constitutive effect of discourse, nor viewed as a robust source of input for the language being called upon to transport meaning in a data collection-analysis-research result production process.

With this view of language as a perspectivator there follows an awareness of a need and a fruitfulness around the use of alternative vocabularies and the assessment of these in terms of what various language uses will simultaneously reveal, conceal, and make possible and impossible in terms of data production and lines of interpretation. Such a use of alternative vocabularies means that empirical indicators – interview statements, observation protocols, questionnaire responses, documents – are opened up to alternative representations and under-standings. As empirical material has then no definite meaning, it can be used for alternative purposes, including the generation of different interpretations and the stimulation of different ideas.

The Consequences of a Constructionist Position

In this book, we emphasize researcher constructions and wish to underscore the possibilities of taking options and responsibilities more seriously than is common, where data are reported as if these mirror the world. Of course one could say that research, and in particular interview work, is about co-construction in the sense that the researcher and the interviewee will interact closely and produce 'knowledge' or at least the raw material for knowledge, jointly (Miller & Glassner, 1997). But in the end, the researcher must be responsible for the constructions claimed to be research contributions. Even if he or she sees him- or herself as a microphone-holder and/or a conversa-tion recorder, this responsibility can't be avoided. Who is allowed a voice and whose rhetoric (claims to knowledge, to reveal authentic experiences or emotions) is central in a research document, comes down to researcher choice. Giving/neglecting/marginalizing/reinforc-ing voice and also giving indications of the validity/value/relevance/(dis)respect are key (political and ethical) issues which the micro-phone-holder can only pretend to bypass or minimize (Alvesson, 2002).

The various turns or passages where construction work is done are important to consider. If one looks closely at the research process, there are further constructions after the construction work that is carried out in interview settings or in producing observational protocols. These fur-ther constructions (coding, interpretation, analysis), or re-constructions of the social constructions, are produced or read into the lives of those studied – and also known as 'data'. The systematic exploration or at least serious consideration of a variety of 'native-constructions' and 'researcher-constructions' then offers various possibilities (and perhaps some pain) to researchers trying to open up material for novel and surprising constructions. As with our entire approach this is in opposition to most uses of grounded theory, phenomenology, and other inductive approaches. Through multiple readings we increase the chance of encountering/ producing unexpected constructions – opening up rather than letting common sense (as in grounded theory) determine 'reality' – and also the chance of establishing that the unexpected is not just the outcome of a specific and narrow way of seeing.

Theories are helpful here in making construction work more well-informed, conscious, and nuanced. Theories of use in construction work on 'data' can be understood as repertoires of lenses (Deetz, 1992), in that each provides and communicates particular understandings that are closely contingent upon the chosen vocabulary and its use in context. This metaphor points out the productive and pragmatic characteristics of language. Language is a human artefact that affects our vision – blurring, clarifying, magnifying, and diminishing the things we can see through it. From our point of view, theories do not express the underlying engines of generalized empirical patterns. Rather, they are instruments that provide illumination, insight, and understanding. In this sense theories operate as idealizations (Freese, 1980). But as instruments they are difficult to use in an incisive way. They can't be fully controlled as it is impossible to freeze-frame meaning. Our use of theory and language is better seen as a struggle. Our conception of theory may be looser than the mantra of explicitness, abstractness, discreteness, systematicity, and completeness. It is, however, probably more realistic and most likely also more useful – as Shotter (1993: 113) points out, few, if any, theories can meet these criteria.

From this perspective, empirical evidence is constructed within particular paradigmatic and linguistic conventions and is typically less robust when approached from any other angle (Gergen, 1978). At the risk of repeating ourselves, most interesting (complex) ideas cannot be easily 'checked' against data and empirical measures are always contestable. Families, occupations, workplaces and firms, for example, are complex, dynamic, and difficult to observe. Employing different languages produces partly different empirical materials and reality by its nature does not simply invite and make self-evident the use of a particular set of words to describe itself. What, for example, is to be

QUALITATIVE RESEARCH AND THEORY DEVELOPMENT

seen as an occupation is seldom beyond dispute. That we talk of university teachers – and would include everyone from senior professors at elite institutions (leading PhD seminars and supervising PhD students in nuclear physics) to junior assistants who are working in vocational training (say with nurses at a teaching-focused institute) – may indicate something homogeneous, but this is simply one effect of using this term rather than giving us something that reveals anything about the reality 'out there' with regard to practices, meanings, relations, and material conditions. That a wide variety of people can be said to be university teachers may in one sense be 'true' but it is also misleading, while the choice of using such a category may be a bad analytical choice, involving the closure and homogenization of what should remain open and diverse.

Without advocating solipsism, relativism – in the vulgar sense of any truth claim being equally (in-)valid – or an exclusive focus on the rhetorical qualities of research texts and theories, we think there are good reasons to move away from:

- a strong focus on data towards an interest in the construction of empirical material;
- a view of theory and data as separate towards an acknowledgment of the 'internal' relationship between them and the theory-impregnation of all data;
- a strong emphasis on the procedures and techniques for 'collecting' and analysing data towards a greater interest in researcher reflexivity in dealing with the empirical material, i.e. in how to interpret and reinterpret material.

From this perspective, acts of construction – always guided by theory in some form – become central. The knowledge and the person doing the knowledge work/development can't be separated (Calás & Smircich, 1992). The framework, the researcher, and the social reality while inescapably represented through potentially contested representations are thus always interrelated and provide an interconnected net of potential insights and ideas, ideally cultivated through discipline and self critique (c.f. Mills, 1959; Weick, 1989). Reflexivity then enters the picture (Alvesson & Sköldberg, 2009; Calás & Smircich, 1999; Hardy & Clegg, 1997), pointing to the struggle to acquire an awareness of how paradigms, socio-political contexts, frameworks, and vocabularies are involved in the shaping of the researcher's constructions of the world at hand and his/her moves in doing something with it.

Theory as a Vehicle for Disclosure

From all of this, it follows that in this kind of work *an open attitude is crucial*, but that this is very hard if not impossible to accomplish. The challenge – one calling for much more than good will and theoretical ignorance – is to open oneself up to a variety of possibilities.

A research approach which tries to accomplish a high level of openness has perhaps been best described by Deetz (1996) as a local/emergent research orientation. Deetz contrasts *elite/a priori* and *situated/emergent* research perspectives. The former (admittedly extreme) position means that a researcher starts with a set of concepts *a priori* and applies them to whatever field he or she deems suitable for the purpose of testing the theory at hand. It is the theory that matters and the field simply provides the possibility to test it. Whatever else the field provides is of no significance or interest since the research design only permits the field to say 'yes' or 'no' to the theory (often via a set of hypotheses). The situated/ emergent position means providing 'a participatory ethnographic rearticulation of the multiple voices of a native culture' (Deetz, 1996: 592). In this case, the researcher aims towards a hermeneutical translation and clarification of the life-world of the particular group of people under study. This ideal may be reframed as in the postponement of closure in the research process as well as in the written text.

Here, of course, it is important to *avoid* the naive idea of being 'non-theoretical' or blank as a means to being open, as implied by some views of grounded theory (e.g. Eisenhardt, 1989; Glaser & Strauss, 1967). This simply means that cultural taken-for-granted assumptions and other implicit theories will take precedence. Illiteracy does not lead to an open mind. Openness, a consideration of alternative routes of interpretation, and analysis are better accomplished through our familiarity with an extensive repertoire of theories and vocabularies that can be used reflexively (Rorty, 1989). In terms of gender, for example, 'openness' is not just a matter of making gender visible through observing sex differences ('body counting') or through paying attention to the espoused meanings and experiences of men and women. It involves questioning these two seemingly homogeneous categories and paying attention to various forms of cultural masculinity and femininity, with the possibly shifting character of these cultural meanings in local contexts and the ways in which they inscribe a particular order on the world. It also means an openness towards how researchers may order the world through constructing it in terms of masculinity and femininity (Alvesson & Billing, 2009; Ashcraft & Mumby, 2004).

Openness is thus not a matter of avoiding theory or postponing the use of it, but instead demands that we include a broadening of the repertoire of vocabularies and theories that can be mobilized in order for us to consider more and less self-evident aspects. A particular interpretive bias, following on from a closed theoretical/ cultural/ private orientation, may be counteracted. Theory is often seen as providing direction and control, but it can also be mobilized as a *tool for disclosure*. A theory can open up not only other theories and their lines of interpretation, but also sensitive constructions and interpretations of empirical material. In relation to Deetz's categorization, this view slices through the intellectual terrain and the ingredients slightly differently, as some (but flexibly and (self)critically used) elite/*a priori* elements are needed and must be used actively in order to accomplish a better emergence. There is of course a dilemma here regarding the use of *a priori* in order to accomplish emergence, as the former potentially includes both an emergence facilitation as well as a blocking of elements.

Care in employing or accepting conventional words here may be helpful. Concepts such as leadership style, motives, services, men and women, childhood, class, innovation, learning and so on do not of course necessarily prevent phenomena being productively interpreted in these terms. It is however likely that what is conventionally and commonsensically labeled using these terms may sometimes be more productively interpreted by means of other terms. Obviously, one can always question the value of general concepts – and the problems raised by references to the commonsensical ideas and prejudices associated with the signifier should not be underestimated. However, it is also important to recognize that the linguistic ambiguity of broad concepts provides unifying symbolic functions for researchers; 'they are robust mechanisms for generating scientific communion' (Astley, 1985: 501). As such they work on the social level to control commitment and mindsets. Some willingness to work, not only intellectually but also socially, against forces encouraging us to pre-structure what we find at the same time as we believe we are open is necessary. We need to use various resources in our struggle to open up our orientations. We will discuss some of the interpretive principles that are helpful in this respect in the next chapter.

THE ROLE OF CONSTRUCTIONS AND LANGUAGE IN EMPIRICAL RESEARCH

Summary

In contemporary social science there is an enormous amount of varied stances on constructionism (Alvesson & Sköldberg, 2009; Steier, 1991). We do not concern ourselves here with different claims about the social construction of reality type (Berger & Luckmann, 1967) and instead are more interested in how researchers will always construct the phenomena they are studying. We must, in a sense, invent the world we are trying to understand. And this is the case even if we (we think) have the deepest respect for reality, if we try to be as open-minded as possible and are eager to minimize the impact of specific assumptions, theories and models. The risk of relying on such openness is that we are instead naively guided by taken-for-granted assumptions, un-checked theoretical ideas and lines of reasoning ingrained in our cultural and scientific traditions which we never make explicit. Commonsense reasoning is not the same as intellectual openness.

Against a conventional view of language as a transparent medium for the transport of meaning, critics have emphasized its ambiguous, metaphorical, context-dependent, and active nature. Language use produces as much as it reveals of the world. The language used in a study will influence the results – and unduly so, if it is not capable of taking the relativity, the selectivity, and the ordering-effects of vocabularies seriously and critically into consideration. Language is tricky and relative and this is the case for researchers (and their research vocabulary) as well as for informants (and their everyday use of language). Language provides a layer of meaning for extra-linguistic realities, thus making these intelligible and communicable. However, different vocabularies will produce different understandings of the 'same' phenomena – all are potentially 'true' but not necessarily commensurable. This indicates the importance of an access to and a willingness to consider alternative vocabularies and to explore how they can lead to constructions of (partly) alternative realities (Rorty, 1992). Postmodernists would claim that our efforts to say something definite, to establish how things 'are', rely on shaky foundations and ought to be deconstructed. This includes showing the false robustness, the contradictions, and the repressed meanings within statements. Minimally this may prove a useful exercise, perhaps stimulating new ideas.

Our overall suggestion in this chapter (and the book as a whole) can be summarized as follows: it is better to work with flexible and varied

QUALITATIVE RESEARCH AND THEORY DEVELOPMENT

constructions rather than trying to build a solid ground, and to see language as something that can always actively portray reality as carrying a specific perspective as more insightful than viewing language as a passive medium which mirrors the reality 'out there'. Working empirically should not mean that one tries to let 'data' point at a relevant use of language – this is the core idea of general ideas about the importance of using codification in analyzing 'data' and also the use of computer programs for sorting material – but rather one should more actively and creatively use a variety of vocabularies for creating possible meanings out of the empirical material. As the meaning of the latter is never given, active work is necessary with this. As the establishment of a specific truth is almost always doubtful, other more imaginative uses of empirical study as well as a theoretical elaboration could be up-graded.

3

KEY METHODOLOGICAL PRINCIPLES
FOR DETECTING MYSTERIES

If knowledge is socially constructed and developed, as we have argued in Chapter 1 and Chapter 2, how should one proceed? In this chapter we point to five interpretative principles that are of particular value for constructing and solving mysteries. Research is often seen as an enterprise searching for patterns. Important traditions will typically assume and then tend to find some fairly clear pattern. It will be taken as the norm that there are experiences shared by groups of females, that managers have specific leadership styles, and that there are cultures made up of webs of shared meanings that will create coherence within a collective. This is fine, but in order to use empirical studies as a way of challenging established concepts and knowledge it is important not to assume too much from patterns and to avoid underestimating the potential of addressing social phenomena in ways that will break with how we tend to order the world. A key capacity of and interest in mystery-creating research is refraining from habitual pattern-inscribing work.

In this chapter we deal with patterns and ways of avoiding or minimizing this privileging of pattern-seeking. We argue against the setting in stone of empirical material, at least too early on in a research process, where the researcher wants control and therefore underestimates the value of allowing the empirical material to surprise. One key aspect here is to counter assumptions about patterns with ideas about social reality being more fragmented – at least in relation to the type of patterns that are assumed. Important in the breaking away from easily recognizable patterns is the ideal of research as defamiliarization, i.e. turning the well-known and self-evident into the opposite, into something exotic, strange, and non-natural. This is closely related to the idea of problematization, implying a willingness to suspect the self-evident and useful, and calling for the examination of whether seemingly good starting points and vocabularies can really help understanding. Problematization calls for but also means and facilitates creativity. Problematization is facilitated by switching between looking for/(re)constructing fragmentation/patterns and defamiliarization, but also by efforts to back up these operations with theoretical resources. We shall talk here about developing broad scholarship and reflexive critique – this means the active and systematic use of a set of theoretical ideas and vocabularies in interpretive work.

In this chapter we therefore address five methodological principles that we think facilitate the construction and resolution of mysteries:

- *(De-)fragmentation* – producing an interplay between pattern- and fragmentation-seeking, without necessarily seeing the former as the end result (or at least not the only end result) of a good study.
- *Defamiliarization* – trying to refrain from using familiar concepts and frameworks and instead opening up the studied reality as an unknown and unfamiliar place.
- *Problematization* – the unpacking, deconstruction, and critique of concepts and categories that belong to the received cultural and scientific traditions and wisdoms, and that also form the major input for our thinking and construction processes.
- *Broad scholarship* – to develop and maintain interpretive repertoires, and to emphasize that while observations are theory-laden, there are always excesses at the margin that cannot fully be captured by an interpretive repertoire, and that different interpretive repertoires will cast empirical observations in different lights.
- *Reflexive critique* – the conscious effort to open up and consider alternative ways of working with these issues, e.g. through invoking alternative metaphors and vocabularies.

We illustrate these principles through a case study of leadership in an organization.

(De)fragmentations: Working with Patterns and Fragmentations

For many researchers pattern-seeking is the key point of science. The enterprise is about finding patterns, whether these are about recognizing causal effects, mapping the world, or pointing to a deep meaning in a text. Finding or even inscribing patterns is not in itself wrong, but often our expectations or vocabularies will mean a premature ordering of the phenomenon to be addressed. (Just labelling about a phenomenon can often mean such an ordering and is seldom unproblematic.) Such a tendency can be found in both map-the-gap and discovery studies, but also in much interpretive work. Here it is common to look upon the material under study as text, indeed as a single (holistic) text. One can imagine interests in a diversity of patterns, but our point is here to argue for a reduction of the faith in and focus on finding patterns. A pattern-seeking approach is not the only one imaginable. To continue the text metaphor, one can contrast this with ideas about a variety of texts that have been written and re-written in a variety of ways. These can then be seen as starting points for understanding the individual subject, the workplace, family, career path, occupation, or region to be studied. The non-obviousness of meaning as well as the potential of multiple meanings – ambiguity – are emphasized.

The interest in finding (constructing) deviations from patterns implies a search for (opportunities to come up with) fragmentations. Incoherencies, paradoxes, ambiguities, processes, and the like are certainly key aspects of social reality and worth exploring – both as topics in their own right and as a way of getting beyond premature pattern-fixing and the reproduction of taken-for-granted assumptions about specific patterns. But here we don't have in mind a celebration and privileging of fragmentations and ambiguities. Rather it is the dialectics between patterns and fragmentations that are of interest. The researcher will try to go beyond the 'surface', in opposition to both a positivistic (data collection) and a postmodernist (focusing on signs, liberated from meaning and depth) preference for avoiding interpretation. She or he will look for something less obvious or less easily revealed in a (quick) coding process. The text as a totality is also carefully borne in mind. This means that variation and contradiction are seriously considered, and not suppressed or neglected (c.f. Potter & Wetherell, 1987).

This combination means that analysis will include activities of pattern-inscribing/interpreting as well as of fragmentation-inscribing/ interpreting. It will consider constructing order as well as disorder. This then means that the work will include considerable efforts to interpret 'deeper' meanings, to look for contradictions as well as patterns, coherencies in incoherencies, puzzles, and so on in empirical material. This way of looking at empirical material means that its dialogic qualities are emphasized. The researcher must call upon or actively try to reach

QUALITATIVE RESEARCH AND THEORY DEVELOPMENT

empirical material that can produce – or inspire the construction of – a variety of alternative 'stories', or at least the inspiration for this. Thus the process of engagement, in which the languages and theories of the researcher are activated, is central rather than the passive mirroring of reality (e.g. through collecting data and coding, processing, and trying to 'discover' what is there).

This view is different from most conventional approaches, guided by a wish to order, control, and domesticate what is studied. But the impulse to control – through measuring, codifying, checking, and so on – can be bracketed, and a desire to become challenged, surprised, bewildered, and confused may take centre stage in research. The researcher's preunderstanding, and the academic framework(s) s/he thinks s/he masters, may be invoked as a participant who is open to a dialogue and a more or less radical rethink through the encounter with empirical material. Before this is packaged (codified, categorized) serious attention will be paid to whether it can be unpacked instead. The combination of a fairly sophisticated, but unfixed preunderstanding and empirical material constructed in non-trivial ways – through these preunderstandings and the use of theoretical ideas and methodological principles – provides the basis for theoretically innovative work circling around (de)fragmentation (Alvesson, 2002).

Commonly-used vocabularies, codifications, and categories do not reveal the truth. They can at best assist us in developing frameworks and describing phenomena so that knowledge providing insights about the world can be developed. 'Categories' here refer to concepts seen as being capable of assisting the sorting and naming of the chunks of reality studied by a researcher. They will typically privilege overpacking and invite pattern-seeing. Family, identity, decision making, organization, society, political parties … these terms all encourage finding patterns. Categories impose order; they structure the world according to a particular logic. Categories are not only valuable tools for understanding but also mechanisms for power and control that can fixate our ways of seeing. They are not so much sources of misunderstandings as basic ingredients in forms of understanding that are insufficiently problematized and give too little space for uncertainty and variation. This chapter addresses how the categories forming basic elements in the formulation of research questions, structuring the field, working theoretically, analyzing empirical material, and arriving at conclusions, call for careful scrutiny. One possible antidote here is the upgrading of fragmentation as a value, but there are other 'positive' reference points (e.g. defamiliarization).

Defamiliarization

A particularly important element in critical research is to avoid seeing the social world as self-evident and familiar, and instead to conceptualize it as basically, or in certain vital respects, a rather strange place. Research then becomes a matter of defamiliarization, of observing and interpreting social phenomena in novel ways compared to cultural dominant categories and distinctions. Defamiliarization means that we see things not as natural or rational but as exotic and arbitrary, as an expression of action and thinking within frozen, conformist patterns (Alvesson & Deetz, 2000; Ehn & Löfgren, 1982; Marcus & Fischer, 1986).

This is indeed a difficult enterprise. Researchers, like other members of a society, are trapped by cultural ethnocentrism and parochialism – meaning that the cultural phenomena they encounter are not recognized as such, but are seen as natural, as part of the world order, and not bound up with national or late capitalistic/post-industrial society and culture. Gregory, an anthropologist working in the organizational culture area, remarks that the literature often says 'more about the culture of the researchers than the researched' (1983: 359). This kind of research problem is more generally recognized by anthropologists (Marcus & Fischer, 1986). And going somewhat further, some proponents would warn against the study of one's own society. Leach, for example, writes that:

> ... fieldwork in a cultural context of which you already have intimate first-hand experience seems to be much more difficult than fieldwork which is approached from the naive viewpoint of a total stranger. When anthropologists study facets of their own society their vision seems to become distorted by prejudices which derive from private rather than public experience. (1982: 124)

This is bad news for anthropology and other forms of cultural research that have increasingly targeted social groups within researchers' own society during the last decades. Culture – including taken-for-granted assumptions and ways of thinking – is, however, not the only element in our inclination to reproduce a well-known world in research. The other issue is language. We create and recreate familiar words through using language in conventional ways, where the terms we adopt will guide our perceptions, descriptions, and interpretations. This is unavoidable. We have no other choice than to use the tools that are at hand.

But this does not mean that we have to subjugate ourselves to preformed meanings and understandings uncritically and unreflexively. The way forward is to choose one or a few dominant categories in the field one is working in, and to then start by investigating its (problematic) restrictive impact and in the process perhaps indicate challenging ways to approach the subject matter. If this is done well, it can in itself be a valuable research contribution.

Problematizing the Taken for Granted

Simply replacing a familiar category with something that makes a phenomenon less self-evident is one principle, but one may go beyond (or not as far as) that and emphasize the re-working of an assumption, theory, or concept instead.

How does one problematize a dominant category or idea? Problematization means that more effort is put into thinking through what may be rethought in terms of assumptions, ideas, and the conceptualization of a particular subject matter. It is thus something different from puzzle-solving work (Kuhn, 1970). As we see it, problematization first and foremost involves a systematic questioning of some aspects of received wisdom in the sense of dominant research perspectives and theories (but also of the subject matter itself), while at the same time offering a 'positive' or constructive formulation of interesting research questions. The way we define problematization here then also differs from critique or deconstruction or reflexivity, although these may be major elements in (resources for) the process. Critique is a major element of the problematization project, but here it is seen as a means rather than as an end in itself. In efforts to open up and scrutinize established thinking, critical frameworks can be used as methodological resources.

The concept of universities may be instructive. A university signifies a place where mostly good things happen: the production of knowledge and learning, the facilitation and active encouragement of free and creative thinking, the provision of qualifications and skills, the guardian of enlightened meritocracy, and so on. In a university there is research and education – and also perhaps some administration. It may not be a total surprise that we have strong sympathies with these rose-tinted sentiments – and to some extent we also think that these are more than half true – since both of us have chosen to take up employment there. Universities are indeed places where good things happen, more or less. They are in the knowledge and intellectual qualification business, making people and society more knowledge-able, qualified, and competent.

But the list above certainly does not exhaust all plausible (true) characterizations of universities. For example, although students may well tend to like the commercial benefits of qualifications and skills, they might be more inclined to think of the university as a place where they can live a hedonistic lifestyle in total abandon at very little cost. For students, the lofty ideals of enlightenment provide more of a hazy background to rounds of parties, exams, and boundary-testing experiments. The end product – a more mature and well-rounded person or a hedonistic one (not oriented towards making too much of an effort and avoiding unpleasurable duties) – may be or not be valuable to society, but this has very little to do with knowledge production, free thinking, and meritocracy. Another option is to see the number of people in higher education as a matter of performances in an (imagined) international Olympic games of higher education statistics: the ambition here is to place oneself as highly as possible, win glory, and achieve pride as a true knowledge holder within the most educated proportion of the population. Whether the statistics will say anything about educational level in a more qualitative sense is, of course, a completely different matter. But this is difficult to assess and easily lost from us so the symbolism of high numbers easily becomes an objective in itself.

Society – to be read here as various leading actors – may also have a hidden agenda. Although it certainly tends to subscribe to enlightenment values publicly, it may also find universities attractive because they are a fine place to store people that otherwise would end up in problematic sociological categories: as unemployed, welfare recipients, deviants, or even criminals. (Alternatively, those being at the university for a few years may reduce the competition for employment, making it possible for other people to get jobs and thus be preoccupied in ways that do not create social disorder.) From society's point of view, the main benefit to universities may be that they take care of problematic people: it is the place itself that matters and not what actually is going on (although it may be decisive that universities have worthy causes). Here universities emerge as gigantic car parks or substitutes' benches, perhaps so that as the economic life cycle changes they can be absorbed on the labour market.

Considering these various views of the meaning of contemporary higher education implies that one should be careful when assuming that the label 'university' is a concept that is particularly valuable for understanding what goes on. Similarly labels like education, learning, research, and knowledge production should be used with care. These may all prevent us from producing interesting ideas about the phenomena we may be interested in investigating. Too much is easily assumed and the outcomes of studies will to some degree be givens from the start if one is studying the university as a site for education and research. It makes sense to assume that certain things that can be interpreted in line with these terms can also be detected, but it is far from evident as to what the labels actually refer to and often other things may prove more salient or interesting to bring forward. The academization of some occupations aspiring to become 'real professions' does seem to lead to various efforts to produce PhDs where the research element is a bit odd given the conventional definitions. Perhaps legitimacy and status here matter more than knowledge production?

Moving this macro-oriented effort to consider various overall conceptualizations of the world of schooling closer to specific sites of qualitative study, we can, following Thomas, problematize the classroom setting by invoking a variety of alternative considerations for understanding what takes place there:

> Classrooms are no longer a congregation of learners receiving information from a teacher, but a microcosm of discrete and overlapping manipulative struggles for status, respect, and sexual conquest, as well as ethnic hostility, degradation rituals, facework contests, and power-domination games. (1993: 44)

This is an example of a fairly broad-brushed, *a priori* problematization, where the basic meanings or root metaphors for a particular kind of institution are considered and then reconsidered when the object of study is being theorized or defined. Established meanings can and should be questioned (and possibly re-considered also) before and outside empirical inquiries, but as our task in this book is to suggest ideas for how empirical studies can inspire a rethinking of conventional views, an example of an empirical study being helpful seems to be required. But problematization can also take place on the micro level, e.g. in interviews where the researcher-interviewer does not accept the ideas and line of reasoning of the interviewees, and instead draws attention to dilemmas and encourages a rethink and learning (Kreiner & Mouritsen, 2005).

Broad Scholarship – Developing
and Maintaining Interpretive Repertoires

We would label the set of perspectives, concepts and themes that a researcher masters as an *interpretive repertoire* (Alvesson & Sköldberg, 2009). Such a repertoire includes the paradigmatic, theoretical, and methodological qualifications and restrictions that guide and constrain research work. (We use this term differently from Potter and Wetherell, 1987, who refer to a repertoire of words. We are interested in the cognitive capacities.) The interpretive repertoire is made up of theories, basic assumptions, commitments, metaphors, vocabularies, and knowledge. It indicates the 'academic' part of researchers' preunderstanding and the entire spectrum of theoretical resources that may be put to work when researchers confront empirical material marks the limits for what researchers can do in terms of creating something out of certain empirical material, material that in itself has been produced based on the interpretive inclinations of researchers. It also offers input to the struggles inherent in, as Becker puts it, 'getting control over how we see things, so that we are not simply the unknowing carriers of the conventional world's thoughts' (1996: 8).

The interpretive repertoire is made up of elements of relative degrees of depth and superficiality. Of course, few people can master a broad spectrum of theories in depth. There are few really open-minded scholars and some of those that do exist are perhaps not interested in empirical studies or will choose to emphasize the creative aspects of research. At one extreme the researcher will have a firm grasp of some theories and discourses and can therefore use them skillfully. At the other extreme, the researcher will have a mere familiarity with other theories and discourses and can therefore only apply them in a crude and uncertain manner. We can refer to these end points as the deep (or scholarly) and the shallow (or lay) elements in the repertoire. Deep elements are central to the interpretive repertoire and may be easily activated, whereas shallow elements may be described as crude in terms of mastery and peripheral in terms of interest and awareness. Typically, researchers will have a strong tendency to use the deep elements of their repertoire since there is a likelihood that these will lead to results, albeit in a rather predictable way.

The shallow elements in the interpretive repertoire are only activated in research work if the empirical material obviously appears to be in line with these elements. This typically indicates that the empirical material is seen as important or interesting when framed in this way. Researchers will have three alternatives when they believe that the empirical material has triggered thinking, activating the shallow/ peripheral elements in the interpretive repertoire: a) to drop the theme; b) to refer to it briefly or mainly in empirical/low-abstract terms; or c) to develop the relevant parts of the interpretive repertoire and then conduct a more advanced investigation of this phenomenon. The third alternative means that the shallow part of the repertoire stands more centre stage and researchers must develop their skills in using it, thus moving it to the deeper part of the repertoire. In such a case, empirical material will typically have the chance of making a real impact on the research outcome. What is important in the present context is sufficient familiarity with a theory (perspective, discourse) to be able to consider it; a willingness and potential to develop knowledge; and enough time and flexibility in the research process to use this knowledge, even if it had not been initially intended to play a direct role in the project.

This ambitious use of the idea of an interpretive repertoire is necessary to inspire a self-critical use of theory in which empirical material and alternative theories can be employed as elements in theory-development. Carefully constructed empirical material is utilized in order to problematize a targeted theory, thus opening it up for re-considerations and alternative understandings. In organization studies the work of Morgan (1980, 1997) has been vital in this regard. In addition, the literature advocating multi-paradigmatic studies is relevant here (e.g. Gioia & Petre, 1990). One can debate the extent to which it is possible to cross over and master several paradigms (Burrell & Morgan, 1979; Hassard, 1991; Parker & McHugh, 1991), but we would agree with Lewis and Grimes (1999: 686) that 'exploring "foreign" paradigms offer theorists a potentially "frame-breaking experience"' that challenges an established position and encourages rethinking. One can also imagine the same effect through the use of less divergent approaches than those associated with different paradigms. If this inter-theory challenge interacts nicely with the empirical material, the likelihood of a productive breakdown in relation to empirical material increases. The combination of questioning in empirical experience and inter-theory confrontation gives input for the rethinking of a particular understanding.

Reflexive Critique

Perhaps one of the most valuable lessons from the modernism-postmodernism debate is that the ideal of a well-integrated theoretical frame of reference should be treated with caution. It should also be recognized that such frames of reference can impede our understanding and also mislead researchers or readers as a result of their totalizing effect and their tendency to present reality as unambiguous and accessible to representation in the chosen theoretical idiom. Rorty warns against an approach in which a 'final vocabulary', a language providing the ultimate knowledge or wisdom, is used. Instead he proposes a position in which the researcher 1) 'has radical and continuing doubts about the final vocabulary she currently uses, because she has been impressed by other vocabularies...; 2) realizes that arguments as phrased in her present vocabulary can neither underwrite nor dissolve these doubts; 3) insofar as she philosophizes about her situation, does not think that her vocabulary is closer to reality than others, that it is in touch with a power not herself' (1989: 73).

An openness to the appreciation of the values and limitations of different vocabularies and understandings is thus well motivated. There is something to be said for being beware when it comes to 'monologic texts (that) employ a consistent and homogeneous representational style ... and express a dominant authorial voice' (Jeffcutt, 1993: 39). This lesson can lead to a certain modesty when confronted by the idea that truth, or the 'right' or 'the best' interpretations, can be produced. In such a case a greater willingness to allow diverse vocabularies, interpretations and voices to make themselves heard in research texts appears to be preferable. As the knowledge and the person doing knowledge work/development can't be separated (Calás & Smircich, 1992), reflexivity is called for (Alvesson & Sköldberg, 2009; Hardy & Clegg, 1997). One possible 'focus' here is on the preunderstanding/theory/fieldwork/empirical construction interface(s), namely on how these elements closely interact, overlap, trigger each other's 'presence', and thus can't be reduced to separate, discrete entities in the research process. Preunderstandings, in combination with access to formal theory and a research vocabulary, guide fieldwork and produce certain empirical constructions. At the same time fieldwork experiences selectively trigger associations and connections that are not inseparable from preunderstanding and how theory is invoked and framed in the local context.

It is, for example, important to realize that researchers will primarily use those theories they have grasped very well and for which they feel an emotional preference. Very few researchers can successfully shuttle between theories with different paradigmatic roots. It is possible to operate within a particular intellectual horizon, which may incorporate some related intellectual traditions. If we broaden our horizon in

QUALITATIVE RESEARCH AND THEORY DEVELOPMENT

one direction, it is not unlikely that we can narrow it in another. However, researchers may also conduct secondary or complementary interpretations taken from frameworks or positions within the set of theories to which they are mainly committed. By making comments from alternative positions, it becomes possible to cast a critical light on the set of perspectives favored, and to encourage the reader to consider yet more alternative interpretations, thus further counteracting the totalizing element that is more or less pronounced in all research, and about which postmodernists are with some justification so worried.

One illustration of reflexive critique is to try to conceptualize empirical material in terms of the various logics this may express. When considering statements from research subjects – whether in interviews or observation – these can be seen not just as possibly revealing the meanings coming from those studied (or facts about their organizations), but also as political action, moral story telling, identity work, script application, and so forth (Alvesson, 2011). Rather than assume that the subject is reporting authentic experiences, we can see the subject as a politically motivated producer of what are for her/him favorable 'truths' or as a person repeating institutionalized standard talk about a specific theme. Thus, interview talk can be seen as useful for a study of political action or the circulation of discourse rather than for a study of the experiences, meanings, and beliefs of individuals. Great care must be exercised before a researcher chooses a particular construction.

Even if a researcher is well versed in the particular theoretical positions used in a multiple interpretation framework, it will still take a lot of re-reading for them to change from working with one theory to another. An exposing of the gaps within a particular, favored line of inquiry is also often time-consuming and stressful. Moving to a new position calls for an 'unlocking' and a desocialization from the previous position. It is necessary to distance ourselves temporarily from the theory in which we were previously engaged. Perhaps the research process should be divided into distinct phases. Paradigmatically-related theories can make changes possible, but may also make it difficult to exploit any differences fully. It is like speaking two similar languages. The similarities make it easier to get a fairly good understanding of both of them, but they also often make it more difficult to master either one completely, as it is so easy to mix and confuse the two. Never underestimate the hard work involved when using several theories at the same time!

We should also add here that the very point of using multiple interpretations is that each should add value. It is unsatisfying just to add on greater numbers of theories and vocabularies in order to introduce possible ways of understanding subject matter – each proposed under-standing must include a creative idea. As it is sometimes difficult to come up with a single really, or even a moderately, good idea when working with empirical material, it is obvious that multiple interpretations not only involve quite a lot of theoretical and analytical work, but also call for a lot of inspiration and luck.

An Illustration: Studying 'Leadership'

The five interpretive principles of (de)fragmentation, defamiliarization, problematization, broad scholarship, and reflexive critique can be illustrated through the example of researching leadership (or 'leadership', as we sometimes see and label it), which we happen to have studied. Leadership is useful in this context, since it is both evergreen and fashionable, anchored in our everyday language, and yet sufficiently complex to be worthy of scientific exploration. It has recently gained greater currency, both in popular and academic discourse. In one of our case studies – originally aimed at exploring the aspects of knowledge work – we encountered unexpected and also confusing interview accounts on leadership (a more comprehensive discussion of the case can be found in Alvesson and Sveningsson, 2003). This prompted us to pay this greater attention.

In this scenario a number of senior managers at a pharmaceutical company were asked 'What do you do?' as an initial, opening-up question. Almost all claimed that they did 'leadership'. We will only mention one example here from the entire study. When asked to specify what he meant by this, one manager said:

> … my view is that it is teamwork and everyone is important, everyone is needed. OK, key scientists are important … we must be prepared to reward them in a whole new way compared to what we've done before. To me it is extremely important to emphasize the team, the whole team. If you have an idea and you are unable to execute it, it is worthless. I've got plenty of ideas and I'm going around and spreading these among people. But one thing which I think is important from a leadership point of view is that those responsible for the projects can also decide on which ideas they want to pursue. It's not me who should tell them that. I tell them the ideas I have and often they will say 'That's no good, so we don't like it'. And that's perfectly OK for me. Sometimes they will think it's good and then they will adopt it. But the important issue is that they as a group decide by themselves to carry on. (Manager A)

Is leadership patterned? This statement on leadership indicates that the manager (in this case superior to the project manager) participates in discussions and offers ideas, but without any persistence or eagerness to make the team respond. There is no asymmetry or privileged direction-provision involved: the manager places himself on the same footing as the others. There is also a rather strong abdication from decision making: in terms of leadership what is important is that those people who are responsible for projects must decide. The meaning of leadership in this case seems to involve abstaining from taking a leader's position.

It is also worth noting that the interviewee goes back and forth in emphasizing the key part of all this activity. The first sentence states plainly that this is teamwork: each person is vital. He then says that 'key scientists' are important, which must by definition be true ('key' implies 'important'), and underscores this by claiming that they must be rewarded in a completely different way than had been previously done. This seems to be a strong statement in favour of the value of key scientists to the company. But the entire team then re-enters the picture, with formidable strength: 'for me it is enormously important to emphasize the team, the entire team'. This team then seems to overtake the key scientists in the interviewee's ranking. The account, as we read it, is incoherent: the key scientists, in particular, should be rewarded (presumably far more than the rest) and the entire team should be emphasized. This indicates a shifting and indecisive (or perhaps flexible) view on how 'leadership' is to be exercised. One can thus make a case for some degree of fragmentation and processuality in the meanings surrounding leadership, thereby counteracting efforts to fix the subject within a specific style or coherent view.

Defamiliarization and problematization. Not only this person but almost all the managers we interviewed put forward a notion – or several versions – of leadership in accordance with contemporary fashionable scripts for how one should conduct leadership. In this respect all the managers appeared fairly well informed and progressive. However, when asked to outline the topic their views of 'leadership' became vague or even self-contradictory and the initial positioning almost melted away. At the end of most of the interview accounts, there was not much 'leadership' left intact. It therefore appears reasonable to not accept the conventional ideas about leadership and management as preached by an enormous amount of leadership studies, but to see all this as quite strange and exotic. Why are those studied so eager to try to present themselves as 'leaders' and why do they have problems in doing so in a way that hangs together? Rather than seeing their 'performances' in this respect as indicating problems of competence – the result of bad management development practices – one could turn a critical eye on the notion of leadership as expressed in academic and other settings.

If we use even moderate criteria for coherence, clarity, links between ideas and practice, and a certain level of ambition for something we would label 'leadership', there are still reasons to doubt its 'existence' in the case above. We suggest that mainstream ideas about leadership (as expressed in the leadership literature and among practitioners) may assume too much. At least in our study it seems often very difficult to identify any specific relationships, behavioral styles, coherent view, set of values, or an integrated, coherent set of actions that will correspond to, or can be meaningfully perspectivated, as leadership in a significant and intended form. We thus arrive at the conclusion that there is not necessarily much 'leadership' produced in many situations and that established notions about the self-evident nature of leadership call for a rethink.

These ideas are backed up with broad readings of a variety of literatures, encouraging a breaking out of conventional, neo-positivistic, as well as meaning-centered ideas on leadership: a broad *interpretive repertoire*, in which not only a set of leadership approaches but also other perspectives on language, subjects, social relations, ideologies, and discourses (ranging from discourse analysis, symbolic interactionism, poststructuralism to critical theory) can offer a wider perspective on how to interpret talk about leadership. Assessments of the relevance of these various intellectual resources are not to be made *a priori*, but the use of ideas is to be partly guided by empirical impressions. When we thought that interpretations were deviating from conventional assumptions – and partly from what we expected – some poststructuralist but even more identity ideas were brought into the research process.

Important here was the use of *reflexive critique*. Because it appeared that dominant leadership ideas – as taught in executive development programmes and propagated by business magazines and consultants – had been accepted by the senior managers studied in a rather incoherent and loose way, we carefully thought about this in order to make sense of (as well as produce) interesting new ideas on these. Various theoretical sources of inspiration were considered, including Foucault, which would say that subjects were being constituted by the leadership discourse. But as their grip on the subjectivity was quite loose, and the power/knowledge connection and normalization effect did seem to be surprisingly weak, we resisted the temptation to employ this seductive theory.

Our purpose with this exercise is not to demonstrate 'how it really is' with 'leadership' in a specific company (or perhaps in large parts of contemporary organizations) – in fact, we think that 'how it really is' can perhaps only be established on relatively trivial matters – but rather to show how established ideas can be challenged and rethought. We realize that talk about leadership is altogether difficult to avoid: it is too deeply ingrained in cultural understandings of modern society, with strong colonizing effects. A refusal to reproduce some of these understandings may lead to marginalization or even to being expelled from the good research community. There is a very large leadership industry within and outside academia and most people who have built their careers and lives on leadership (not 'leadership') are not easily convinced about the discourse informing managers' talk and the kinds of identity struggles that can have a clear bearing on their practices. Partly as a consequence of cultural domination, both in institutionalized settings (education) as well as everyday working life, these categories have certain steering effects that are difficult to avoid. One possibility here is the use of alternative and varied vocabularies (e.g. 'influencing efforts' or 'organizing' instead of 'leadership'). One could imagine texts alternating between the familiar and defamiliarizing vocabularies, thus encouraging our liberation from conventional wisdom, without necessarily alienating us totally from mainstream concerns and risking us having no dialogue or impact with representatives of the dominant views. The simple signifier 'leadership' with its problematization and defamiliarization ingredients to some extent points in this direction.

Conclusion

We started this chapter with a caveat against focusing too much on pattern-seeking in research. This does not mean that we are against searching for patterns. Obviously, many if not most research aim to identify logics, regularities, principles, or other pattern-like entities. Hence, the impulse to look for patterns and regularities in empirical material is easy to understand and is also normally something that would facilitate analysis. In a broad sense, an emphasis on 'anti-pattern' aspects like fragmentation or ambiguity will also include a component for patterning – to make a case for position-shifting or indecisiveness also includes an element of pointing at patterns, in a loose sense.

However, a one-sided focusing on pattern-searching in the traditional way is less helpful if one wants to challenge dominating logics and perceptions about the morphology of the present – that is, the shape of things as we understand them today. Rather, it is important to apply tools that will help us to identify and clarify the problems associated with particular ways of representing reality. In this chapter we have offered five methodological principles to facilitate this kind of enterprise (de-)fragmentation, defamiliarization, problematization, broad scholarship, and reflexive critique.

Together these indicate how one may proceed in order to counteract the very strong inclination to use established and dominating assumptions, categories, and lines of reasoning. Of course it is impossible and probably unwanted to counteract all of these. The 'successful' researcher would most likely produce the experience that this is absurd and unhelpful rather than interesting and productive (Davis, 1971). The purpose of this book is not to promote postmodernism but to stimulate an approach where we may engage empirical material in unexpected ways in order to develop new ideas. And trying to accomplish less closures and a greater opening up of routes for some unexpected lines of enquiry can be a fruitful way forward. This may indeed be necessary in order to create interesting and theoretically novel ideas.

QUALITATIVE RESEARCH AND THEORY DEVELOPMENT

A METHODOLOGY OF SORTS FOR
THEORIZING FROM EMPIRICAL MATERIAL

The overall purpose of this book is to suggest a methodology (overall principles as well as a design) for research that aims at producing new empirically-supported theoretical ideas. Crucial here is improving the chances of formulating interesting and challenging revisions of dominating ideas. In previous chapters we have outlined some general views on the nature of empirical material and methodological principles for reducing the risk of uncritically reproducing established wisdoms and instead opening up empirical impressions for novel thinking. We now move further to suggest and specify the metaphor of theory development as mystery creation and solving work. We also offer a methodology for how to proceed with this in the research process.

Before doing so we will briefly discuss the question of what is interesting in research and examine the importance of recognizing the social dimensions of research, supporting and disciplining the researcher who is relying quite heavily on subjectivity.

What's Interesting?

What is an interesting research problem? As we see it, this must include the potential for novel insights that will add significantly to – or goes against – previous understandings. It should thus include something unexpected and challenging; something that turns at least some elements of earlier knowledge on their head. Normally something interesting will also mean clear connections to what is (perceived to be) socially and practically relevant and recognizable, but also something having a broader theoretical relevance. For example, this may mean allowing for and encouraging abstraction, aiming for in-depth understanding, and now and then attempting to provide explanations for the phenomena of which the focal empirical case is one example. Contrary to conventional wisdom we think that it is fruitless, and even counterproductive, to attempt to minimize the influence of theory and the researcher's subjectivity in direct work with experiences and initial interpretations of empirical material, i.e. we don't believe in the theory-data separation. After all, you can't count heads without having a theory of what a head is and why it is worth counting in the first place. Subjectivity should not be denied and hidden, but rather it should be reflexively and self-critically cultivated and mobilized, reinforcing the ability to discover interesting research issues. As Weick puts it,

> Whenever one reacts with the feeling that's interesting, that reaction is a clue that current experience has been tested against past experience, and the past understanding has been found inadequate. (1989: 525)

In order to make this experience more valuable and relevant, it must be abstracted and made more general. More specifically, we would suggest that theory-developing social research can be characterized by working with research themes that can be empirically investigated: empirical material that carries some credibility, meaning that it is capable of offering up clues for thinking and the making of claims and/or counter-claims. This work should be conducted in ways that can open up for and encourage those ideas that will offer challenges to conventional thinking within an area, pointing out any shortcomings or paradoxes. This requires an intensive empirical material/theory interplay where theory is also used 'negatively'. A significant resource here is theory (models, vocabularies) that fails to be useful in accounting for a phenomenon, as this will give us a starting point for rethinking. This does not imply a Popperian ideal of falsification, but can still be seen as a chance for problematization – a vital element in theory development as we see it (Alvesson & Sandberg, 2011).

The inference mechanism that guides this kind of theory development is usually labeled abduction (Peirce, 1978). As pointed out by Van de Ven (2007: 98): 'Problem formulation and theory building follows an abductive form of reasoning, which is neither inductive nor deductive. Abduction begins by recognizing an anomaly or breakdown in our understanding of the world, and proceeds to create a hypothetical inference that dissolves the anomaly by providing a coherent resolution to the problem'. Abduction consists of three steps: 1) the application of

QUALITATIVE RESEARCH AND THEORY DEVELOPMENT

an established interpretive rule (theory); 2) the observation of a surprising empirical phenomenon – in the light of the interpretive rule; and 3) the imaginative articulation of a new interpretive rule (theory) that will resolve the surprise. This approach includes an interest in the problematization and re-thinking of dominating ideas and theory, when empirical impressions encourage such a need for novel thinking. The rationale for this is that

> the contribution of social science does not lie in validated knowledge, but rather in the suggestion of relationships and connections that had not previously been suspected, relationships that change actions and perspectives. (Weick, 1989: 524)

Interesting research thus means a new angle, a new connection, which breaks with established knowledge and ideas, and that, as Davis (1971) expresses it, challenges established assumptions (or at least weakly held assumptions). This is something else and more than just a fine-tuning or expansion of earlier theory. It is, at heart, an attempt to re-think conventional wisdom and challenge dominating theories.

Dialogue Qualities Challenging Assumptions

This way of looking at empirical material emphasizes its dialogic qualities, where it is not the empirical material in itself as much as our (research community's) assumptions about what we should try to understand as sufficiently important to consider. A good dialogue will include adopting careful listening, making statements triggering responses, and being willing to take those responses seriously. A good dialogue will also include – or will produce – unexpected statements and bring about learning. Researchers must call upon or actively try to reach empirical material that can produce or inspire the construction of a variety of alternative 'messages', with some of these upsetting their assumptions. Thus the process of engagement, where researchers actively deploy vocabularies and theories, is central. As we pointed out before, this view differs from a position that aims to mirror reality passively – e.g. by collecting data and coding, processing, and trying to 'discover' the facts and meanings that are assumed to be already present.

The proposed view (sensitive constructions) is also different from most conventional approaches, in that it is not guided by a desire to order and control what is studied. For many definitions of science this

A METHODOLOGY OF SORTS FOR THEORIZING FROM EMPIRICAL MATERIAL

desire is central: it is associated with rigor and rationality. Order and control facilitate monitoring and replication, which are key virtues according to the positivist legacy. However, it is possible to bracket this impulse to control – through measuring, codifying, checking, etc. – and instead to let a desire to become challenged, surprised, bewildered, and confused to take centre stage in research.[1] Researchers' pre-understanding (including their academic framework(s)) may be used as a tool that will open up a dialogue with the empirical material. This dialogue needs to include the reader. Intuition and the experience of this are interesting and vital, and the element of subjectivity is also strong here.

This approach gives considerable space for researchers' subjectivity – a preunderstanding, imagination, a feeling for what is interesting is important to acknowledge and use – at the expense of plans, proce-dures, and techniques. The latter is of great importance, but in research aiming at developing ideas these are not to be privileged. An important question and an exercise in reflexivity in the research process is to ask oneself: 'Can I construct/make sense of this material in another way than that suggested by the preferred perspective/vocabulary? Can I let myself be surprised by this material?' But this 'I' needs to be supple-mented and backed up. In a later instance it is vital to make sure that this surprise is not simply a personal reaction that is due to limited empirical experience and theoretical overview. One should therefore ask: 'Can others in the research community also be surprised? Can the empirical material productively and fairly be constructed in a way that kicks back at my framework and how we – in my research community – typically see and interpret things?'

---

[1] We realize that there are many ways in which researchers from different camps and with various personal convictions will work. Some people in associating themselves with grounded theory would probably share Strauss and Corbin's (1990, 1994) beliefs in objectivity, reproducibility, and unbi-ased data collection providing a robust base for theory building, while others would open up for more constructivist considerations (Charmaz, 2000). A strict focus on coding would probably for most mean a minimiza-tion of researcher subjectivity for the benefit of reliable procedure. One may, however, work with coding in different ways; perhaps do multiple codings, based on re-readings and re-framings of one's position; take inco-herences and contradictions seriously; and generally try to open oneself up to experiences of productive breakdowns. But a strict and ambitious codi-fication project, where the faithful representation of data is the key virtue, is very different from the research ideal suggested here.

Disciplined Imagination

Of course, all this leads to considerably more freedom when compared with an approach of trying to stay very close to the data and to see the latter as providing the robust building blocks to theory – to be a creative thinker rather than a 'code-slave' (obeying the commands of the master data). This does not mean that a researcher will have a licence to follow any creative hunch. Still, the empirical material has a very important and critical role as a dialogue partner, putting considerable constraints on what can be done with particular material.

Mills (1959) and Weick (1989) suggest that theorization is best understood as *disciplined imagination,* namely as an effort to find a good compromise between the two ideals making up this conceptualization. Empirical material is particularly helpful within this understanding of theorization because it provides resources for both imagination and discipline. It is a resource for imagination because breakdowns in pre-understanding stemming from the empirical material will create spaces where imagination can be put in play. The field can also provide ideas that will stimulate the imagination, in particular in terms of challenging the conventional wisdom.

Importantly, empirical material also provide discipline. Although empirical material never exists outside of interpretative repertoires, it nevertheless creates an outer limit for our imagination. Some constructions make more sense than others. Those concerning empirical raw material will appear more or less relevant and appropriate and further constructions trying to further refine the material also may be more or less well supported by it. Empirical material anchors the process of theorization in specific claims about the object under study, thus disallowing arbitrary and far-fetched ideas to be put into play.

Although the approach suggested here veers somewhat more towards imagination than discipline, it is important to avoid getting caught up in personal and idiosyncratic views about what is interesting. Our point is that we do not just encounter empirical material and then see where it leads us. We need to use our imagination in order to avoid falling into predetermined codifications and categorizations and as a means to consider the whole variety of possibilities. Often several possibilities of interpretations will be possible, and in a sense we need 'discipline' not only in order to avoid 'non-grounded' ideas but also that we may move beyond the habitual reproduction of a dominant framework and vocabulary. Imagination in this sense is not just tempered by 'discipline' but also presupposes it. The latter then is about imposing constraints on wild ideas as well as against habitual lazy thinking and categorization.

Thus empirical material, when properly constructed, helps form a strong impetus towards rethinking conventional wisdom, but the ideal is *not*, as in neo-positivist work, to aim for an 'intimate interaction with actual evidence' which 'produces theory which closely mirrors reality' (Eisenhardt, 1989: 547). The empirical material should be mobilized as a critical dialogue partner and not as a judge or a mirror, which problematizes a significant form of understanding and thereby encourages problematization and theoretical insights. This metaphor for fieldwork – critical dialogue – frames the enterprise quite differently when compared to the conventional wisdom, as articulated by Eisenhardt (1989) and others following grounded theory thinking.

The social aspect of the dialogue researcher – empirical material

It is extremely necessary here to consider also the collective forces that are directly and indirectly involved in research. Social links and mechanisms will typically temper researchers. Researcher subjectivity – including intuition, imagination and a feeling for what is interesting – is fueled by academic training and scholarship, at least for those with a fairly high level of competence and a degree of maturity. The researcher is normally a part of a broader 'we', which will include the research community (or communities) that s/he belongs to and which inform pre-understanding and preferences. Our experience of 'that is interesting' is typically not idiosyncratic but instead reflects a collective pre-understanding. A qualified researcher's personal subjectivity is thus not quite so central as those ideas that s/he shares with others in the same research tribe and which may often be confused with objectivity and/or a superior way of understanding a phenomenon, being beyond serious questioning. (In this sense, we should be less worried about subjectivity than about collectivity – and the conflation of consensus, objectivity, and valid knowledge.) How this community is targeted, convinced, and challenged is a key issue in doing fieldwork, interpreting empirical material, and even more so in the crafting of a text. The case for something being interesting must undergo peer scrutiny, which will inevitably involve some measure of disciplining efforts.

Our understanding of research is that this is very much a social and political process and very seldom something carried out by the autonomous researcher acting in splendid isolation, liberated from political forces operating directly or, and more often, indirectly. Our references to pre-understanding, theoretical frameworks, and vocabularies point at the social nature of all research, as these are hardly individual inventions or expressions of idiosyncrasies but part of research as a collective project. One always belongs to an intellectual tradition and a community that will include, but not be exhausted by, interactions and dialogues – with colleagues at conferences, within research groups, with journal editors and reviewers, and so on.

This shall include both negative and positive elements. The socialization and mainstreaming effects reduce our imagination and make for a lot of research that reproduces the dominant assumptions and vocabularies. Positively, there is often a strong quality-reinforcing component to be found here. The research community will regulate and cultivate subjectivity and offer counter-points against bad ideas and arguments.

The social and communal dimensions of theories also mean that the individual researcher is clearly linked to broader concerns, such as cultural frameworks and norms, and not only primarily to subjective and personal concerns. We want to emphasize the necessity of relating breakdowns and mystery candidates to the theoretical and empirical work of others. Even though a major part of the dialogue will be between the researcher and the empirical material, the social nature of research makes it imperative for the active individual researcher to keep in close contact with published research findings and public opinion on the matter at hand. By doing this, she or he also widens the dialogue so that issues about what is interesting, surprising, and a potential theoretical breakthrough take into account other voices from the research community, as well as from practitioners and others who may have something relevant to say.

A Mystery Creation and Solving Approach

We have thus far developed our view on empirical material as a dialogue partner and emphasized that the space allowed for researcher subjectivity will be tempered by social forces – namely socialization effects and the pressure for norm-following, as well as social discussions about ideas and interpretations. It is now time to move on and examine our root metaphor for good social science: mystery.

The road to mystery is, however, filled with not only good intention, but also with breakdowns in understanding. A few words about this key step before exploring this view of mystery are called for here.

A METHODOLOGY OF SORTS FOR THEORIZING FROM EMPIRICAL MATERIAL

Breakdowns – spontaneous and created

In ethnographic work within anthropology, the initial difference between the traditions involved (the researcher's and the object of study) more or less automatically produces breakdowns in understanding (Agar, 1986): there is a lack of fit between cultural and theoretical expectations and actual experiences. Researchers will resolve this problem by trying to understand the cultural elements that are causing the breakdown, and then adjusting the research schema. Breakdowns will continue to appear until researchers can fully understand the studied culture. This means that ethnography can be described 'as a process of coherently resolving breakdowns' (Agar, 1986: 39). Knowledge is produced along the way, although this is often a more 'substantive' knowledge of the empirical domain than a theoretical knowledge that possesses more general relevance. The idea is often one of rich description.

When studying relatively familiar phenomena (like workplaces, families, social welfare policies or gender issues within one's own country) the problem is often not only or even primarily resolving breakdowns, but there is also typically an element of *creating* them that is necessary. If we accept the socially constructed nature of social reality as well as research, this creative element is always involved. However, more efforts are called for in studies of fairly familiar phenomena within one's own broader culture than in those of more unfamiliar settings, even though one will occasionally encounter original and exotic phenomena in one's homeland also. 'Homeland' here is hard to define – nationality and region are key aspects, but class, work area, gender, ethnicity, etc. also matter and are sometimes even more important to consider. There are no simple formulae for what is a familiar *vs.* an exotic terrain. Male researchers studying female professionals might involve a strong overlap (in terms of class), while female researchers studying, say, prostitutes may encounter a clash of frameworks. (Some older feminists used to emphasize women's unique and shared experiences, assuming that there was much in common in being members of the 'the second sex', but today variety is emphasized and the idea of talking about sex/gender as a fixed and uniform category has been rejected.)

The trick when there is a strong familiarity between the researcher's and the studied's orientations and habits is to locate one's framework (cultural understanding) 'away from' the cultural terrain being studied, so that enough significant material can emerge to resolve the breakdown. This is of course to a large extent a matter of creativity, but it is also a matter of wanting to achieve 'anthropological' rather than familiar or 'technical-pragmatic' results. To some degree it is a matter of using the critical strategy of de-familiarization, as mentioned in Chapter 3: 'Disruption of common sense, doing the unexpected, placing familiar subjects in unfamiliar, even shocking, contexts are the aims of this strategy to make the reader conscious of difference' (Marcus & Fischer, 1986: 137). But the other, related interpretive principles of (de)fragmentation, problematization, broad-ranging scholarship and reflexive critique will also support this ideal of creating (candidates) for breakdowns. Apart from general intellectual efforts to engage in 'deep thinking', one can employ such tactics as using unconventional and varied literature, drawing upon personal and research experiences that are different from those that were salient in a previous study, and putting together a research team so that different viewpoints (and thus different inclinations to see a variety of familiar and unfamiliar aspects) are represented. A mix of people in terms of class background, gender, ethnicity, political affiliations and age may be beneficial here, although a diversity in viewpoints may also create problems of cooperation.

A breakdown in understanding represents an excellent opportunity to start a process of theoretical problematization. The experience of 'What goes on here? I don't understand this!' is a good point of departure. Of course, we are not referring to the lack of understanding that is an effect of not grasping the technicalities of a production process or a craft, or the specific local conditions associated with people and their history and relations in a village or a family. This is a breakdown in the sense of a deviation from one's theoretically informed expectations that are themselves fueled by cultural and academic knowledge. It is the deviation from expectancy that is of interest. However, in order to be of value to research it must be grounded in a cultivated framework – a preunderstanding that is anchored in theoretical knowledge and a familiarity with earlier studies. Working actively with breakdowns as a major element in the research process calls for a sorting out of sophisticated breakdowns from those breakdowns that are contingent upon ignorance with a particular site: only the former has a potential theoretical value while the latter may be important for the sake of ethnographic description. In fields with which we are too familiar, we may need inspiration for the creation of breakdowns, i.e. by challenging our basic assumptions and letting the world surprise us, in ways that hold potential theoretical interest.

Mystery

As stated above, many breakdowns are not of sufficient interest to qualify as key ingredients in the process of formulating a mystery.

Many are temporary effects from a lack of sufficient familiarity with the studied setting and will disappear during the process. Others will remain despite more observations and interviews and will call for our analytical effort. A mystery is thus an effect of several and/or repeated breakdowns, plus our consideration of a more theoretical nature. The establishment of mystery calls for a careful mobilization of existing research results and relevant theory, i.e. a good grounding in the research literature. But this grounding is of course to a large extent 'negative': of interest here is the mystery that challenges existing theory and calls for new ideas. It is the aspects of a theory that do not work that are of interest. Broad scholarship, including an ability to use a variety of perspectives and reflexive critique, is crucial here.

A mystery must always be seen in relation to something in addition to the empirical observations (constructions) that will provide a reality-based inspiration for its construction. It is a mystery given a certain set of assumptions or line of reasoning. It also means kicking back at a set of established knowledge. Problematizing the latter and making it non-familiar to the empirical material is then an important ingredient. The latter provides a point of departure and offers resources for crafting the mystery: something that is unexpected must be seen in relation to what is expected, and having a set of assumptions and truth claims associated with a theory is helpful in the articulation of why something could be seen as a mystery. A mystery as defined here is always theoretically informed and calls for theoretical development in order to 'solve' it, i.e. create a good understanding of it, which does not involve application but a significant revision of existing theory or the development of a new theory.

At the same time, a good mystery should also have relevance outside of a given, perhaps narrow framework. The development of interesting results should be acknowledged as valid and important from more than one point of view, i.e. it should go beyond a piecemeal adding-on to a specific, specialized theory. For many economists deviations from a maximization of self-interest or a premium on monetary rewards may be mysterious, but for most of the rest of us it would perhaps be more of a mystery as to why people would maximize their self-interests or view money as the most important thing in life. Mystery *formulation* calls for the targeting of a theory (framework) that will offer a point of departure and reference point in mystery creation (the Other of the mystery), as well as a (brief) consideration of other relevant theories.

It is a delicate matter here as to what degree one should engage with a broader set of theories. At one extreme, one can find (i.e. construct)

QUALITATIVE RESEARCH AND THEORY DEVELOPMENT

a mystery that is clearly rendered and interesting from the viewpoint of one tradition but less of a big deal within competing theories. The risk is a too narrow and limited theoretical development within or in relationship to existing frames of reference. At another extreme, one can find something that is generally odd and unexpected but there are no theories that have really dealt with the phenomenon or offered a good reference point, therefore making the mystery less easy to formulate and any theoretical contributions more difficult to make. Constructing a good mystery is thus not easy, but an awareness of these two 'traps' and care in navigating between specificity and broadness in the use of a set of theories can be helpful here.

A Loose Design for Exploring Mysteries and Breakdowns

Although the overall idea of constructing and solving a mystery through working with breakdowns is sufficient as a methodology, it is not that easy as considerable support is needed. In Chapter 3 we pointed towards some useful interpretive principles and in this chapter we have explored how to consider the dialogic nature of empirical work that is aimed at producing interesting results through disciplined imagination. But all of this can be supplemented with ideas on what the specific research process, involving various steps or moments, could look like.

The meta-framework outlined above offers broad guidelines and direction but, crucially, is not 'locked' into a narrow way of seeing that determines the results *a priori*. This makes it possible to work with a more technically specific method/research practice that structures the dialogue between theory and empirical material, in which the pre-understandings, expectations, and imaginations of the researcher are crucial. The key elements here are finding ways of encountering breakdowns and creating mysteries. Below, we outline a method for doing this (also, see figure 4.1 for a visual representation).[2]

1. *Familiarization with the setting under study and making inquiries about themes in a fairly open way.* This is based on preliminary decisions

---

[2]This is a full version of the ideas we are advocating. We here assume the possibility of having close contact with and going back and forth to the research site. As pointed out above, breakdown-oriented research can be associated with the use of any kind of method, and can also be used in more moderate ways, but for reasons of clarity and space we concentrate here on one version only.

A METHODOLOGY OF SORTS FOR THEORIZING FROM EMPIRICAL MATERIAL

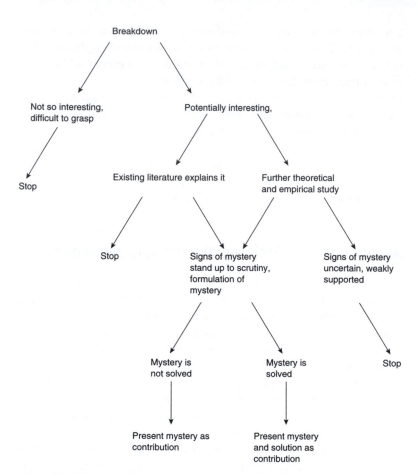

Figure 4.1 The research process: a simple version (from Alvesson, M. and Kärreman, D. (2007) Constructing Mystery: Empirical matters in theory development, *Academy of Management Review*, 32: 1265–1281. Reprinted with permission from the publisher.)

about a field of interest and an initial, fairly broad focus for the investigation. Rather than focusing on narrow themes e.g. 'knowledge sharing', 'teamwork' or 'leadership', one can ask oneself 'What is going on here?' or 'What do the natives think they are up to?'

The main problem with starting with narrow themes is that the guiding assumptions will become a strait-jacket for fieldwork. If one wants to generate rich empirical material that allows for symmetrical claims on the levels of talk, meaning and practice, one also has to provide enough space to make it possible to 'follow the animal'. Themes such as 'knowledge sharing', 'teamwork', and 'leadership' are not ideally

QUALITATIVE RESEARCH AND THEORY DEVELOPMENT

suited to this kind of open-minded research strategy. They assume that there are things like 'knowledge' being 'shared' and that this is significant, that people congregate in teams and that this makes a difference, or that there exist appointed/formally elected 'leaders' or other people who do 'leadership' that is targeted at people who then (mainly) function as subordinates. Problematization and (de)fragmentation should be part of a researcher's mindset.

Obviously, a study must have a degree of direction. The trick here is to balance this with a capacity to expose oneself to the unexpected, the stuff that can't easily be disciplined by the preferred vocabulary and framework and too narrow a research question. One may, for example, start with (but not necessarily stick to) an idea of 'knowledge' being 'shared', workers horizontally coordinating their work, or managers exercising influence over the meanings of their subordinates and then see what may turn up – what one may produce – in terms of unexpected empirical material, in that kind of area, broadly defined.

It is important to view such assumptions as starting points. This means that their usefulness may not survive for very long. This is not really a problem: indeed it is at least much less of a problem, in our minds, than staying too long with fairly useless (un-checked) assumptions that will hamper the discovery/creation of interesting empirical material. The key point is to engage in a reflexive use of the initial assumptions. Reflexivity here could involve a critical awareness of the risks of imposing and sticking to a set of favored themes and a willingness to invoke alternative themes, vocabularies, and understandings. Issues around politics and ethics are also likely to emerge in more acute senses: who may benefit from studying a specific set of phenomena in a particular way?

2. *Encountering/constructing breakdowns in understanding.* Fieldwork should be theoretically informed but also varied and rich enough in the sense that it will allow for the existence and exploration of breakdowns. Breakdowns are facilitated through the use of the five interpretive principles suggested in Chapter 3, although these should be applied with caution. The ideal is not to maximize breakdowns through a desire to problematize everything. A really interesting breakdown means that an empirical 'finding' can't easily be accounted for by an available theory. The breakdown is thus *not* the result of researchers' ignorance, naivety or narrow-mindedness. The surprise should be the reaction likely to be experienced by most members of the research community who are supposed to be able to understand/explain the empirical observation/construction triggering the breakdown. It is thus not just the individual researcher but also the collective theoretical and paradigmatic framework and the

A METHODOLOGY OF SORTS FOR THEORIZING FROM EMPIRICAL MATERIAL

knowledge shared within the research community that will be involved in acknowledging the breakdown. Researchers would be wise to make certain that the surprise appears in the context of a sophisticated position and is not partly the outcome of poor scholarship. The surprise should be an outcome of knowledge, not ignorance.

This point may restrict the usefulness of our approach for junior scholars in general and doctoral students in particular. This is true in a trivial sense, but it also over-emphasizes the role of the individual in research. The image of the heroic researcher locked in a struggle for truth in splendid isolation certainly props up much identity work in academia, but it thoroughly misrepresents how research is actually carried out. Experience and overview are helpful – there is no doubt about that – but there are several ways, even for junior researchers, to test ideas in the larger research community. Seminars, workshops, and conferences, and perhaps even more informal conversations, can provide ample opportunities to test whether one's scholarship is up to scratch.

We wish to stress the point of carefully checking on experiences of surprise and breakdown. It is difficult even for an experienced researcher to immediately establish the degree and value of the breakdown that is at hand. A breakdown is experienced personally for the researcher but a more interesting one is also a theoretically validated one. One always starts with a provisional breakdown that must be elaborated upon – its scope and depth, and its relevance for various bodies of literature. In this sense, a breakdown simply does not occur. It is necessarily created by the researcher(s), and ultimately recognized and sustained by the larger research community.

3. *Moving from breakdown to mystery*. After encountering an unexpected finding, the next move will be to formulate some preliminary interpretations of a theoretical contribution through showing; a) the broader relevance of an empirical finding; b) the problems with an earlier theory or critique; and c) some hints of a new understanding through the formulation of the mystery. This phase must include a critical check of whether a breakdown will lead to something new that would be of potential theoretical relevance. Not all breakdowns will allow for the construction of a 'real' mystery. Indeed, most will not. A breakdown may – in the context of this book – be viewed as a mystery-candidate, and a mystery can be seen as the elaboration of a breakdown with a strong potential to offer a theoretical contribution.

A key distinction to note is that a breakdown is mainly of local (empirical site or domain-specific) relevance and can sometimes be overcome through additional empirical work (leading to deeper or

broader empirical knowledge) and/or through consulting the literature. A mystery, as we use the term here, requires a novel theoretical
contribution. In other words, when asking more questions, hanging
around (Dingwall, 1997), and walking to the library to read more
books and talk to colleagues fail to prove enlightening, a mystery is at
hand. Self-critique and reflexivity are important elements here as
antidotes to the tendency to be carried away by the prospect of constructing a true mystery. It is easy to become overenthusiastic about
one's empirical results. Reflexivity may also mitigate the risk of being
insufficiently careful in monitoring the empirical grounding and
potential theoretical value of the claim to mystery.

Again, the research community is an important resource for establishing and recognizing genuine mysteries. Dialogue and conversations with
other researchers are good ways of complementing the individual
researcher's education, and likely to be useful resource to further develop
and elaborate the precise aspects of the mystery at hand. We think that
this resource is often under-utilized, particularly by junior researchers,
who sometimes may feel that they are at risk of being scavenged by
predatory peers and seniors. This is a genuine if somewhat overblown
concern but becomes less of a worry in our approach, since research
predators are unlikely to have uncovered the kind of rich empirical material that is the backbone of genuine mysteries.

4. *Solving or reformulating the mystery through the development of a
new idea that offers a new interpretation of the phenomenon that inspired
the mystery.* Here additional resources, including philosophy and social
theory, are used. This work typically also involves further empirical
investigations, guided by a developed understanding and interpretations supported by the use of additional theoretical and linguistic
resources. Here it is possible to engage interviewees in our efforts to
solve mysteries, through generating ideas and responding to possible
interpretations. (See Chapter 6 for ideas on how to try to utilize interviewees for more analytical and creative purposes than purely descriptive ones.)

Ultimately this step is all about trying to rethink the mystery in a
way that will minimally add to our understanding of its depth and
scope and, preferably, solve it. Useful tools and practices include metaphorization, concept-coining, re-imagining, and synthesizing.
Metaphorization refers to developing particular metaphors that may
shed light on the mystery. A family can for example be seen as an
emotionally strongly bonded mini-community; a consumption unit; a
madhouse where all sorts of neurotic orientations are infiltrated; a legal

entity; and so on. Concept-coining refers to the creation of suggestive names that operates in a demystifying way. Goffman´s (1959) concept of impression management for denoting the desire to look 'good' and save face in everyday interactions is a useful example of concept-coining. Re-imagining refers to the practice of rethinking and redefining old concepts rather than developing new ones. Max Weber was certainly not the first to use charisma as a way of understanding authority, but his usage of the word and his analysis of the real-world phenomenon it purportedly refers to ultimately changed how we understand both authority and charisma. Finally, synthesizing refers to the practice of connecting ideas from different bodies of thought to create a coherent package. Mintzberg's (1979) work on organizational structure and power is an instructive example of synthesizing in action.

To solve or reformulate a mystery typically draws upon our critical use of the interplay between different theories being problematized by the empirical input. One can throw some novel light on the phenomenon indicated by the mystery by using new concepts and a new theoretical framework or metaphor. This can also involve the formulation of new research tasks. The idea is also to transcend the empirically specific and produce something that is of broader relevance. Again, where acts of creativity are central, moments of reflexivity are important for enabling a rethinking of one's preferred positions and vocabularies. In actual practice this step is likely to develop into an extended trial-and-error process and to include several or all of the practices listed above.

5. *Developing the (re)solution of the mystery so that it gains a broader relevance for a specific terrain and this positions it more clearly in relationship to other theories.* This means more systematic considerations of other, but not too diverse, terrains than the one that 'produced' or inspired the breakdown and subsequent mystery. This development may be concerned with theoretical abstraction as well as with considering where and when this might encourage a productive understanding. No theory is always wrong or always right – they will be more or less relevant and helpful in different situations. And it is necessary to have a firm grasp of when and how they may be relevant. At the same time, the approach suggested here is not so much concerned with generalization and abstraction. It is more oriented towards the specific and related empirical terrain that provides the empirical inspiration for the mystery – and thus has a local touch. However, some ideas about the nature of this locality and the kind of domain it may cover are important to establish. This is not just a matter of the type of social phenomena, but also covers time

and history and the relative interpretive value of a theoretical concept or metaphor. All knowledge is preliminary and must be targeted for on-going debate and re-problematization, partly as a consequence of social reality being dynamic.

The mystery approach suggested here is not to be read as suggestive of a final solving of mysteries but as supporting a continuous problematization-oriented view, where the critical dialogue within the research community (and with interested subjects outside it) is a key element.

This list of elements, or stages in work, easily gives a too mechanical or overly structured impression of this process. It is not intended as a manual or a model for how this kind of research could typically take place, although we hope it can be used as a source of guidance and inspiration. As Mills (1959) pointed out, research is a craft. It cannot be reduced to steps, manuals, and models. Imagination, intuition, interruptions, frictions, and creative discussions are vital here and a rigid attitude to plans and steps may prevent this. Because of this, the list above should be seen as a rough description of the elements in research processes that can bring the role of sophisticated pre-understandings and the possibility of a gradual development of theoretical understandings more into focus in fieldwork. One can imagine different modes of working within this framework. Work can be conducted cyclically – one may wish to revisit and reframe the field with a 'preliminarily solved' mystery in order to develop an idea, metaphor or theory. It is also possible that a really challenging encounter could trigger an excellent idea on the spot, thereby making the breakdown-mystery distinction irrelevant and bypassing stages 3 and 4. This is probably less common and a spontaneous development of new ideas is something that is outside the scope of our method: instead we are emphasizing fairly hard work with the empirical material to hand as the means for generating new theory.

Structuring the research process in various ways as illustrated by the model facilitates an interplay between theory, researcher subjectivity, and empirical options that can encourage theoretical development through problematizing existing theory. As pointed out above, our framework is a kind of fuller version that can be associated with field-work and various research methods with a high degree of flexibility. Working with breakdown/mystery ideas in other sorts of research with a more carefully planned, designed and less flexible approach (like experiments or questionnaire studies) may differ in the process. What are important here are the major orientations and not the details of or stages in the research process which will need to be adapted to the specific research design.

Summary

In this chapter we have discussed the meaning of undertaking interesting, empirically-inspired, and supported research. The idea of disciplined imagination is helpful here, although this book pays somewhat more attention to the second of the two terms. The conceptualization of research as the construction and solving of a mystery adds spice and distinctiveness to this general research ideal. Engaging in a critical dialogue with empirical material adds to the set of metaphors, indicating a way of how to approach fieldwork and view 'data'.

As we have (repeatedly) stressed, 'data' offer no reliable signposts, not even after what may seem to be rigorous treatment and analysis. Rather, we are always doing something with data – framing and constructing these. Doing something different to the norm is important in the creativity-stimulating part of research. A careful consideration of alternative constructions is necessary in order to produce a dialogue that may be theoretically inspiring and innovative, transcending the received wisdom and preferred line of constructing.

Working with breakdowns as a key ingredient in the production of mystery (and in its occasionally encountering or, even more rarely, its discovery) calls for a willingness to avoid conventional constructions – aided by (de)fragmentization, problematization, defamiliarization, broad scholarship (mastering a broad interpretive repertoire) and a reflexive critique (see Chapter 3) – and asks us to consider alternative, challenging interpretations of empirical material. The re-constructions emerging from this should meet the criteria of being well supported by the empirical material (assuming that this can support different constructions) and also be found to have some theoretical potential. A serious consideration of alternative representations and interpretations thus becomes crucial in our work with encounters with empirical reality. A willingness and capacity to be surprised, to not just passively wait for breakdowns to occur but to be actively open to these happening, are vital here. Reflexivity can be encouraged by using various theoretical perspectives and metaphors; listening to the alternative voices of research subjects; imagining multiple reader groups; considering different political interests and research purposes (emancipation, thick description, new policies or better management); trying

QUALITATIVE RESEARCH AND THEORY DEVELOPMENT

to consider oneself in various identity positions (gender, ethnicity, class, but also 'type' of researcher); working with co-researchers using another background or theoretical framework; and thus increasing the chances to be challenged when encountering empirical material. The dialogue between framework, researcher, and empirical material should be, multilingual wherever possible.

Working with mysteries calls for much more than rationality and rigor. Using a broad set of capacities and orientations is highly necessary, including imagination, intuition, and a feeling for what is interesting. But as has been said previously, researcher subjectivity needs to be cultivated and disciplined. Access to theory and being reflexive are important. And so is the use of social resources, including the judgment of others within and perhaps even outside one's research tribe (or sub-community).

Researchers will belong to and typically bear the clear imprint of their respective research community. While in fieldwork the dialogue between the researcher and the empirical material is central, behind and also within the researcher we will find a shared social knowledge that is guiding and fused with subjectivity. Continued contact with other representatives of the research community, both through writings of a theoretical and empirical nature and through discussions and assistance with assessments of what is interesting, surprising and novel, will increase the chances of developing broadly relevant contributions. The social side of research is not just positive, but also and always includes the risk of mainstreaming and normalizing both phenomena and researchers. The pressure to adapt to standards and be part of the mainstream is strong. Politics matter here, as many established researchers will safeguard established theories, research programmes, and methods. Nevertheless, it is important to consider also the social dimension of research, which does not work for idea-facilitation alone but also for 'quality' control. Given the loose reliance on procedure and technique in the kind of enterprise suggested here, this element of quality assurance (and discipline) is not insignificant. We need support from others when assessing what is interesting and credible.

In this chapter we have also proposed a sort of design for research that circles around breakdowns and, in particular, mystery construction and solving. Through seeing creative social science as similar to a detective novel and involving these two elements, a view of research as possibly much more imaginative, challenging, and engaging is promoted. Living up to the ideal is not always easy and there is no one set of techniques or procedures that will guarantee the result, although we think the five interpretive principles discussed in Chapter 3 and the

A METHODOLOGY OF SORTS FOR THEORIZING FROM EMPIRICAL MATERIAL

five-step model suggested in this chapter can provide some help with this. The model is intended as a possible supporting structure for the research process. The idea once again is to facilitate creativity and direction, but the decision tree (figure 4.1) also gives some pointers for thinking through those occasions when one should *not* go for the mystery route. Sometimes one's empirical material or ideas can be insufficient. The five-step model can also have some value as a way of accounting for the research process. In qualitative research – in particular, of the type suggested here – providing a clear description of the process can be difficult and the concepts and design for the research suggested here may prove useful. But as stated above, this should not be treated as a blueprint: in a mystery approach specific ideas concerning method must involve a flexible adaptation to the researcher's specific project and local circumstances. How we arrive at a mystery is perhaps in itself often a mystery.

ILLUSTRATING THE DEVELOPMENT AND RESOLUTION OF MYSTERIES

In the previous chapters we have offered a set of metaphors, conceptualizations, and interpretive principles for conducting studies aimed at developing novel ideas through empirically-inspired ways of rethinking phenomena of interest – or phenomena that can be made interesting. How then are the principles for opening up understandings to be applied? How does one work with fragmentation, defamiliarization, problematization, broad scholarship and a reflexive critique? How does one familiarize and defamiliarize oneself with the setting? How may breakdowns be enacted and elevated into mysteries? How might mysteries be solved and resolved? We will now provide some examples of how empirical material can be used productively to rethink and develop theory. We want to stress that we use the examples as illustrations. The point is to show how empirical mysteries can be detected, refined, and resolved.

We shall draw mostly from our own material for obvious reasons. It was clear to us when we did the research that something surprising given the established theories and understandings (i.e. something mysterious), was going on. We believe that in many other research projects empirical phenomena deviating from expectations will also appear and play a significant part in the research process and the production of research results. This is demonstrated through various illustrations in the introduction to this book. However, we have probably worked more systematically and more ambitiously with the approach presented here than most other researchers. Since research reports are rarely fully transparent on how ideas emerged and developed and we lack this kind of access to projects other than ours, we will primarily use our own experience for illustrating our suggested methodology.[1] For each example, we are going to demonstrate how to engage with the steps for mystery identification and construction, as described in Chapter 4. We are also going to point out how to put the various methodological principles elaborated in Chapter 3 into play. The three cases each consist of a study – into gender divisions and identity at an advertising agency; of journalists on an evening newspaper; and of human resource management within a consultancy firm. They are all within our research areas of gender, work, organizations and occupations, thereby covering fairly broad parts of social and behavioral science.

All the examples mentioned benefit from our first step in mystery construction: *familiarization with the setting*. Studies 1, 2, and 4 draw on extensive ethnographic research, where the fieldwork was carried on for more than six months in each case. Everyday interactions, as well as more focused events such as customer meetings and editorial staff meetings, were extensively covered. Interviews with key informants, as well as numerous informal conversations with the 'natives', also provided important empirical material for each study. The third study does not really qualify as full-blown ethnographic work, since the observation part was restricted to around ten episodes, with each ranging in duration from one to two full days. However, this particular study was carried out over four years, and we undertook more than 58 interviews in total, as well as taking advantage of repeat interviews with key informants. All these studies have been published in established journals so we would refer the reader to the full text for more details.

We should also add that the illustrations do not fully demonstrate all the major ideas developed above. There are also some variations in, for example, how a clear construction rather than discovery came out in the cases. Overall methodological principles and the full range of ideas and resources for research work are not always entirely applied in purist ways. There is also always some discrepancy between how one works with methodological ideas in order to be creative and how

---

[1]The contemporary norm in journal publication seems to be the map-the-gap approach, where the researcher identifies a gap in the literature and then tries to fill it. This means constrained, incremental, and non-challenging work and modestly interesting contributions (Sandberg & Alvesson, 2010). It is possible that behind the dressing up of the methodology in this way practices more in line with what is suggested in this book exist, but it is difficult to tell and means that for us it is difficult to draw upon research reports framed in this way.

one fairly effectively and clearly can produce a written account of this. Research needs to be flexible and pragmatic. Therefore if the reader should spot some variations between what has been expressed previously and the applications below, this should not necessarily be held against us.

Case 1: The Play of Gender Stereotypes at an Advertising Agency

The first case concerns an advertising agency (LAA) (for a more thorough discussion of the case, see Alvesson, 1998). The study was initially fairly open, facilitated by the small size of the organization (21 people), but we soon discovered a somewhat extreme division of labour in combination with other interesting gender themes, inviting us to use a gender *metaphor* as a primary *interpretive repertoire*. All the men, with one exception, occupied the professional positions while all the females worked as assistants. In addition, the men were ten years older than the women who were typically 25–30 years old. The females were all attractive and well dressed. LAA was an organization led by men while the women managed routine jobs and the 'domestic chores'.

There was no specific intention to focus on gender issues, but this 'discovery' was seen as a surprise. As such it conforms to *step 2 – encountering breakdowns in understanding*. The gender division of labour – including vertical division – is of course common. One could say that an absence rather than the existence of a gender division of labour would be a surprise. However, the pattern here seemed extreme and unexpected in this kind of work. Advertising is hardly a macho business and one would assume that it would be fairly open to females, especially since the fields of education that are of relevance (communication, language, marketing) attract their share of female students. We had here a breakdown in understanding. This triggered our curiosity and our interest in understanding this case, as well as an effort to *problematize* conventional understandings surrounding the gendered nature of work.

The fieldwork revealed even more interesting and surprising results when the accounts of the men dominating the agency were interpreted. A component in almost any qualitative study is asking about how people see themselves, their work, their relations, and their organization. Interview questions about this, at least initially, will be quite open. In our case we did not focus on gendered meanings, but the way in

ILLUSTRATING THE DEVELOPMENT AND RESOLUTION OF MYSTERIES

which what could be interpreted as such had appeared. The advertising people we interviewed emphasized that they were intuitive, emotional, sensitive to interpersonal relationships, family-oriented even at work, uninterested in their career, part of management, and so on.

> Advertising people are normally very outgoing and emotionally loaded. Because feelings and things like that are the basis of creativity, so to speak. They are often very rich in ideas and associative, they can quickly associate with various phenomena. They are normally rather difficult to steer and jump for joy when they become happy or hit the roof when they become mad. The amplitude of their reactions is much higher than, for example, people who are in companies' accounting departments. Advertising people are seldom very systematic or structured ... (Male advertising worker)

They described themselves, their occupation, and their organization in ways that were firmly in line with cultural views of femininity, at least on an overall and cliché-like level. These statements were also in keeping with the ideals of many feminists based around the importance of emotion and the personal in terms of thinking, work, and organization (Jaggar, 1989; Mumby & Putnam, 1992). Correspondingly, males were conventionally seen to be constructed as non-emotional (Hearn, 1993). Hollway writes that 'in our society, the judgement is a sexist one: expressing feelings is weak, feminine and in contradistinction to men's rationality' (1984: 253). In 'masculine' occupations, jobs will require people 'to be cool, impassive or stern' (Cockburn, 1991: 150). But discourses within the advertising industry will stress emotionality as a core dimension at work, while 'masculine' occupations and organizations will typically do the opposite.

So far we have addressed some fairly straightforward elements of our discovery as well as other clear examples of slightly more awkward constructions in the empirical work. Counting bodies and age differences does not call for much construction work, although putting together a picture of the agency containing older males in senior positions and younger females in subordinate jobs of course involved, a degree of construction. (Based purely on the data, one could have come up with a pattern that people who were taller with shorter hair received messages about greater amounts of money in their bank accounts every month.) More pronounced (sophisticated, debatable) construction work concerned the interpretation of femininity as salient for male advertising staff. Here we would claim that males constructed themselves in a particular way, that these constructions were

QUALITATIVE RESEARCH AND THEORY DEVELOPMENT

accepted (i.e. the researcher saw the words used about emotion, intuition, etc. as indicating meaning and not just jargon), and that they were framed in a specific way by being related to a specific type of literature and vocabulary, i.e. femininity, presumably indicating some deeper insight. Our point here is that this is not just a matter of inductive work, where data clearly showed the right path to knowledge – there was a considerable amount of construction work going on here.

In the study we carefully investigated how such constructions surrounding occupations, the company and the people were constructed in ways that were broadly in line with what could be typically described as cultural meanings of femininity. Several interviews (and to some extent observations) confirmed this. A careful reading of the gender literature also indicated a high degree of consensus on the meanings of such signifiers as emotional, interpersonal dependence, intuition, etc. as signalling something feminine and in opposition to dominant masculinities.

At this juncture we had reached *step 3, a mystery*, or a breakdown in understanding that represents a possible mystery. How could highly asymmetrical gender relations (with men dominating the group) co-exist with 'feminine' values and meanings? Or why was an organization that was dominated by men constructed by them in feminine terms? Further consultations of the gender literature were unhelpful in making sense of this. Gender organization studies generally will emphasize how workplaces dominated by men will be constructed in masculine terms (see Alvesson & Billing, 2009; Leidner, 1991). They do not, on the whole, seem to be able to produce a good understanding of an organization that is extremely strongly hierarchically structured in terms of gender, where men dominate, and where the dominant understanding matches what a large body of literature sees as feminine orientations and values. This exercise in extending and enriching the familiarity with literature that originally was not intended to be central in the study (broadened scholarship) then strengthened the impression that there was an opportunity here to make a contribution.

Literature reviews and additional empirical work further supported the case for a 'mystery'. The case may have been uncommon, but may have still encouraged us to revise some theoretical ideas around the close connection between male domination and the domination of masculine cultural constructions – constructions which mutually supported each other – as had been emphasized by the gender literature. Without denying that this theoretical idea can often make sense, perhaps the case would be able to encourage a problematization and rethinking of gender's operations and the construction of masculinities and femininities?

The mystery in this study was constructed through empirical findings and structured and framed in such a way as to kick back against existing and dominant frameworks in gendered understandings of workplace relations. It is necessary to recognize that this is not a simple case of the data not fitting together with the theory and therefore calling for revisions of the latter. One could have downplayed the significance or relevance of the males constructing themselves and their work in what we saw as feminine terms, and it would have been easy to focus on the gendered division of labour and explain this in conventional ways through referencing male power and homosocial reproduction – with the male founder favoring and working with other males who he perceived as similar and therefore also as easier to work with because he had found them to be more predictable and trustworthy (see Kanter, 1977). However, in the study we found it more interesting to emphasize *defamiliarization*, and not to carry on drawing attention to conventional patterns or to use established explanations. Instead we decided to try to do something with mystery: to construct one and then 'solve' it.

'Solving' this mystery called for us trying out different angles and adopting a wider set of considerations of workplace relations and identities. A key aspect here concerned the character of the type of work studied and relations with clients: these were crucial as well as complicated and for advertising agencies generally often problematical. The case indicated that the link between the construction of an organization in 'feminine' terms and women's positioning was not straightforward. The ambiguity of the work situation, the results, and clients' relations with advertising workers heightened identity problems. As with much other professional service work 'the largely fluid character of anything external to interactional accomplishments, provides for very active symbolic labour' (Deetz, 1997). In this study it complicated gender issues. Construction of the work and organization through the use of an emotionality-intuition-personal chemistry-anti-bureaucracy vocabulary facilitated identity work. It indicated positive values, coherence and distinctiveness, for example in relation to a client's personnel and other conventional people. These were constructed as opposite to advertising people – cautious, bureaucratic, and lacking the right intuition.

What the gender literature would identify as feminine orientations – which it would claim men would avoid and downgrade – was used as symbolic and discursive resources in identity constructions by the advertising people. But the 'feminine' undertone/low degree of masculinity made this solution a mixed blessing. That the advertising agencies appeared as subordinate and 'feminine' in relationship to clients (the relationship was often referred to as a marriage and it was clear that the agency made up the female part) also put some strain on gender identity. In sum, the precarious character of the occupational identity had a clear gendered meaning. From another angle, one could say the gender identity of male advertising professionals was only partially, and in some respects even badly, supported by work, the organization, and client relations.

In LAA, the weak symbolic support for masculinity in the work content and client relations was compensated for by highlighting workplace sexuality and perpetuating internal gender structures. Here the mystery was *re-imagined* as an instance where masculinities could emerge in relation to female personnel, and subjected to what may be conceptualized (*concept-coined*) as 'hyper-femininization'(*step 4*). Gender became structured so that male work/gender identities could be supported. One aspect here was the location of men and women in the division of labour where male power accounted for the recruitment of younger, sexually attractive, lower-positioned women. Another was the heightened state of gender interaction. These two aspects meant that the men could place themselves in 'masculine subject positions', making gender a resource for their symbolic labour, despite the construction of themselves, their work, organization and position in client relations in feminine terms. They 'did gender' (West & Zimmerman, 1987) – that is, they adhered to and reconstructed the norms for acting in line with dominant views on being male – in certain sectors and were then liberated to 'undo' gender in others without too many identity problems. (See Butler, 2004, and Deutsch, 2007, on increased options for the 'undoing of gender' during recent times.)

To conclude the study *resolved*, or rather reformulated, *the mystery* (*step 5*) by suggesting the possibility of a loose coupling between male domination and the domination of masculinities (as these were described in the literature and typically culturally defined). In particular, the presence/absence of specific linkages made by subjects in organizations between what, in the gender literature, was viewed as masculine/feminine properties and the two sexes was important for the fate of men and women. This was partly a matter of power: explicitly labelling what is generally, but not necessarily consciously, seen as culturally feminine may well upset gender orders. In the LAA case, a gender division of labour would have been more difficult to reproduce if the constructions of work content, client relations, and organizational practices had acknowledged a correspondence with what was broadly defined as culturally feminine.

The case presented here provided inspiration for a theory of workplace gender relations that allowed for a discrepancy between abstract ideas of masculine/feminine properties as proposed by gender researchers and local constructions of gender. It also provided a framework for understanding gender stereotypes as resources in social processes, thus illuminating the elastic and relative aspects of gender relations that would enable richer interpretations of their social effects. In short, it stimulated a rethinking of gender from a fixation with how stable and general sets of gender meanings could co-exist with gender domination/subordination sets to an encouragement of how gender meaning could be coupled and decoupled from a vertical gender division of labour. This partly meant the (de)fragmentization of established gender conceptualizations, and the unpacking and partial repacking of new forms of fragmentations and patterns.

Case 2: The News Bill Meeting – Inaction, Non-decision, and Identity Construction

This concerned a meeting that Dan experienced during his fieldwork for his thesis at an evening newspaper (and briefly mentioned in our Introduction). A fuller account can be found in Kärreman and Alvesson (2001). The meeting in question – which the locals called the news bill meeting – was at that time held once every month. Participation was expected from all senior editors, even from those who had a day off. The news bill copy editors also participated, since they, together with the night editors, created the news bills. The meeting took place in territory held by the finance and distribution departments. Since this was a somewhat unusual location for editors to visit, the meeting gained a certain out of the ordinary quality as was signalled by its being in that particular department. The participants themselves added to this impression – no other meeting in the company included almost all the editors in a managerial position, and certainly not those editors who would normally have a day off.

The meeting room would be provisionally decorated with a sample of news bills from the time period that the meeting focused on. Those displayed on the walls had not been arbitrarily chosen. On the contrary, they had been selected because they were believed to represent two important categories of news bills – 'bestsellers' and 'disasters'. 'Bestsellers' were displayed on the wall to the left of the entrance. 'Disasters' were placed on the wall that was straight-ahead of the entrance. To the right of the 'disasters' hung a small collection of 'local bestsellers', namely news bills that had replaced the main news bill in villages, small towns, etc. where this had been deemed justifiable, and that had had a positive impact on sales.

The 'bestsellers' were highly visible, and for everyone to see, telling another story to the one that had been explicitly announced – a story of (relative) sales success. They were arranged according to consecutive days – best Monday was followed by best Tuesday, and so on. A note was attached to each, showing information on its sales in relative and absolute numbers as well as printing duration, i.e. the start and stop times for the printing process. The latter information was held as significant since it was believed to explain variations in sales. If the paper hit the street too late it did not matter what the news bill headline was. The competition – which generally told the same stories, save for an occasional scoop – had already saturated the market. At least, this is what the newsmakers assumed. Printing time was also used to allocate blame – if a print run started late, the editorial department would get the blame since this typically indicated that proofs had been delivered too late; otherwise the printing department would be held responsible for the delay.

The 'disasters' told no immediate story other than one of (relative) sales failure. They are uncovered as the meeting unfolds, adding a dramaturgical effect to the meeting. Shameful 'disasters' were one, if the most visible, of a very few cues that would remind both observers and participants that this was, in fact a staged event. Otherwise, the structure of the meeting was loose and informal, and the atmosphere was casual; friendly, and relaxed.

The proportion between the two categories of news bills was unevenly distributed: 'bestsellers' outnumbered 'disasters' seven to three. Every weekday had its 'bestseller'. 'Disasters', however, had one workday paper entry, one Sunday paper entry, and one holiday paper entry. The asymmetric relationship between 'bestsellers' and 'disasters' was further underscored by the fact that although 'local bestsellers' were displayed, their logical counterpart of 'local disasters' did not qualify as a category. The proportion between 'bestsellers' and 'disasters' was, in a sense, a revealing metaphor for the expected pattern of social interaction during the meeting: both positive and negative comments

ILLUSTRATING THE DEVELOPMENT AND RESOLUTION OF MYSTERIES

were welcome, but positive comments were more welcome than negative.

The meeting had a fairly informal tone. Several separate discussion groups – being as small as two persons, having time-frames as short as one question and a reply, and often including jokes and sarcastic comments – would emerge and submerge during the presentation and discussion of the news bills. Even Hans, who led the meeting, would sometimes engage in 'private' conversations, elaborating and underscoring statements that were made in 'public'. Although the meeting sometimes became somewhat disorganized at a surface level, the issues of news bills, sales, and news making would stay in focus throughout. The general pattern of interaction, except for occasional bursts of discussion and the emergence of separate discussion groups, was that Hans would start to read out loud from the main news bill headlines and the information notes (relative sales, printing times) attached to them, look for local news bills, and then make short judgments on the news bills ('It's a good news bill') and printing times ('Awful late, that one'). This would be followed by the participants also making comments, generally to no one in particular. Then Hans would move on to the next news bill. In some instances, comments would escalate into debates.

The discussions concerning the downturn in sales would be fairly typical. Most staff seemed to believe that the recession was the main cause, together with high rates of unemployment. At least, this was not disputed on this particular occasion. Several argued that the good old days, which in this context meant the late eighties, would never return, and that everyone would have to get used to the present day's sales figures. Manne, the news editor, asked for a historical comparison:

'What year does [our present circulation] compare to? 1968 or -72, or what?'

'Oh no, no', Hans replies, 'it isn't that bad. Well, it isn't really fair, but today's circulation compares roughly to the early eighties'.

'We have never faced the rates of unemployment before, as we do now', Tommy, the night editor, said.

'No, as a matter of fact, the unemployed do not have that much money left', Weta adds.

'They don't have that much to start with', Hans says.

'No', Weta, the sports editor, agrees.

QUALITATIVE RESEARCH AND THEORY DEVELOPMENT

'No money', Hans says.

'It's a goddamn situation, this', Weta concludes. The meeting then turns to
the next item on the agenda.

This event appeared to be a routine affair but it was not that difficult to find it remarkable. Consider, for example, one of the meeting's most striking features – the seeming lack of purpose. One
would typically assume that formal meetings in organizations are
about information sharing, problem solving and decision making – or
at least considerable efforts to accomplish this, even though of course
the complexities of issues and conflicts of views and interests will
often prevent or reduce the degree to which these objectives are real-
ized. If one expects behavior guided by rationality or even bounded
rationality, as most business school students will learn to do, the meeting would surely puzzle the reader. There is hardly anything resem-
bling careful analysis. There is almost no effort to ground opinions in
information. No attempts to engage in decision making to improve
the situation are made. What are the participants – the senior people
in an organization normally seen as populated by relatively qualified
workers – up to? What is the meeting about? Why are a large group
of qualified people so engaged in a business meeting without any
relevant information sharing, analysis or decision making that doesn't
seem to lead anywhere? We don't have to engage in much
de-familiarization work in order to carve this out as an interesting
study. The fact that these are valid questions that do not appear to
have easily available answers means that we have *encountered a
breakdown in our understanding*, thereby accomplishing *step 2*.

To *move from breakdown to mystery*, thus enabling *step 3*, we need to
establish the exact nature of the breakdown at hand. This means
engaging in a broadened scholarship and enhancing and deploying our
interpretive repertoires. Below, we flesh out some possible interpretations of the meeting that draw from relevant stocks of literature, as
well as from the native's understandings of the event. The premise
around which the news bill meeting – at least at a superficial level –
circles, is simple and present in almost every utterance during the
meeting, one way or another: *news bill content sells*. While an external
listener – such as ourselves – may be inclined to understand the relationship between news bill content and sales as highly uncertain or
enigmatic, to say the least, the participants strongly discourage such
interpretations. When the process moves into this direction, where a

news bill assessed as good and the sales of that day are poor, the meeting quickly moves on: a new bestseller/disaster is targeted or the logic of the premise is restated ('good celebrity gossip sells'). A selective use of evidence is invoked. Sometimes participants then run into what is a mystery for them (one can't find any way of accounting for the bad sales following a good news bill) but any potential insight is quickly repressed. The conversation then jumps to the next item.

It is important to recognize that none of the supplemental hypotheses offered were used to replace the premise. They all aimed and were used to create a comprehensible world view where the premise ends up by at least explaining some of the sales variation in a credible fashion – as the marginal variation which is left when one has considered the external and uncontrollable effects of market forces, consumer behavior, the general economy, the weather, the peculiarities of calendar effects, and so on. This variation, they claim, can then be explained by the news bill content. All ad hoc hypotheses presented during the meeting are in defence of its premise. In the end, news bill content sells. It matters. It makes a difference. *We* make a difference.

Why is this meeting so appealing? After all, it is based on a weak premise and provides information that is already known and has been previously distributed to the participants. Most of these have little or no influence over news bills design, which makes the main theme during the meeting more or less irrelevant from a practical point of view. And there are no ambitious efforts to share important information, to make plans to gain better knowledge (e.g. about customers' reactions) or to make good decisions. The instrumental output is non-significant. Why do they bother? Why do people normally working as night editors come to the newspaper at a time when they are free not to participate? And why do all the participants say that this is an important and good meeting?

As Schwartzman (1987) points out, meetings are typically used to make sense of problems, crises, and decisional choices, rather than to resolve them. In that sense, meetings generally operate as sense-making devices. Although we are inclined to accept this as broadly true the news bill meeting still mystifies, thus qualifying as genuine mystery. Little effort is made to make sense of problems, crises, and decisional choices. On the contrary much effort is spent on suppressing any potential problems and circumscribing decisional choices. It is true that the potential for a genuine crisis is voiced, but this does not dominate the conversation, nor does it seem to animate participants' imagination.

We would suggest that the meeting was really about making sense of what and who the participants were in light of their shared work reality. In the meeting the participants explored the meaning of being newsmakers in this company, *re-imagining* it as an exercise in cultural reproduction and identity work (*step 4*). Thus, they explored, elaborated, and fleshed out (aspects of) a shared cultural universe and the social identity of the newsmaker: what being a newsmaker in this company was about, and what consequences there might be. Much of the conversation during the meeting seems to have been about making sense of realities that were external to it – the meeting is, in Schwartzman's (1987) words, the organization writ small. In it, the organization is made visible, i.e. vital aspects of how people frame and synchronize collective action are played out, while assumptions, values, and beliefs are clarified and reproduced.

We would also suggest that organizing can be seen as constructing and maintaining those cultural norms and identities that will facilitate collective action. In the meeting a common identity for newsworkers in this organization was constructed and this happened more or less implicitly. The group engaged in auto-communication (Broms & Gahmberg, 1983): they jointly told themselves and each other 'This is our shared universe, this is how we are', under the pretext of a more instrumental topic. For example, the expression and joint confirmation of the belief 'good celebrity gossip sells' meant a reproduction of the idea that 'We are here to sell, what sells is good, even perhaps trivial phenomena are good to highlight as they sell, while important news, such as serving democracy is not what we do, value or are in this newspaper'.

Brunsson (1985) suggests there is a contradiction between decision and action rationality. He claims that focused and committed action calls for simplified and unreflective decision making, the denial of ambiguity, and a recognition of the drawbacks of a preferred route, i.e. the opposite of decision rationality. Our findings support his thesis that the opposite of decision rationality is not necessarily irrationality. We would, however, be inclined to emphasize identity-regulation as following a specific 'conversational rationality' in terms of aim, means and outcome (*step 5*). The news bills meeting is neither about decision making, nor about preparing for (direct) action. It is about charging a generic work identity – the newsmaker – with local and specific meaning; local enough to make sense of the participant's situation at hand, but not so local that it is incapable of transcending the meeting's horizon.

The meaning of being a newsmaker, as constructed during the meeting, is highly stylized, one-dimensional and bordering on the ridiculous. It is also clear-cut, easy to understand, and has obvious consequences for action. Identity constructions, such as the newsmaker as constructed during the news bill meeting, provide certainty and reduce feelings of isolation and personal responsibility. They also reduce vulnerability in relation to the expectations and norms of other people and groups in the organization. The constructions do not, however, necessarily lead to a stable sense of self or a fixed social position from which to talk and act. Experiences of contradictions and fragmentation, doubts and remoteness, remain part of the newsmakers organizational, occupational, and personal reality.

Case 3: Human Resource Management as Myth, Ceremony, and Identity

In our third case we draw upon a study made of a management consulting firm. Initially this was carried out with the intention of exploring knowledge intensive firms and knowledge work more broadly. However, the ubiquity of the Human Resource Management (HRM) practices in the company was striking very early on during the fieldwork and consequently further engaged our attention. The very first meeting with some representatives of the firm, where they emphasized that 'this is a feedback culture', struck us as interesting. (A full account of the case can be found in Alvesson and Kärreman, 2007.) The firm in question – which we had named Excellence (a pseudonym very much appreciated by people in the company, not surprisingly) – claimed to use a rational and ambitious HRM system by which people were assessed and then developed into a highly competent, motivated, and functioning workforce. People praised the system for its usefulness to junior personnel and also for its capacity to deliver an effective workforce.

However, as one would perhaps expect, there had been a lot of variation in the application of HRM policies, leading to strong deviations from the suggested normative order. This was consistent with earlier in-depth research that had revealed widespread doubts about the rationality of assessment and promotion (Barlow, 1989; Jackall, 1988; Longenecker et al., 1987; Townley, 1999), in favor of emphasizing uncertainties and politics. In a complex, ambiguous world calling for pragmatic behavior, it made sense that HRM practices such as promotion should be loosely coupled with earlier assessments and feedback. Interestingly, the general perception among organizational members was *not* that the HRM system was pragmatic, incoherent, and politicized: on the contrary, organizational members unequivocally expressed a strong belief in the HRM system's capacity to deliver on its promise in a rational and consistent way. They claimed that the HRM system delivered good feedback, fair assessment, input, plus the resources for improvement and meritocratic promotion. They believed it worked. As a consequence, the deviations mentioned above – and fleshed out in detail below – were reported as surprising and puzzling events.

We had a similar reaction of surprise and puzzlement, but with regard to the predominant trust in HRM, which beggared belief and amounted to a *breakdown in understanding* (*step 2*). How could we fathom the finding that organizational members believed in the HRM policies so strongly? Why and how did they not take experiences of its shortcomings seriously? Before we provide an answer to these vexing questions, allow us to provide a brief outline of the HRM system at Excellence. The HRM practices were elaborate and time- and resource-consuming. All employees (even the partners) were expected to take part in various recruitment efforts, such as presenting the firm at universities, interviewing and assessing job seekers, and generally looking around for people to hire. The HR department administered recruitment, but consultants decided on who would be employed. The firm was generally understood to be a career firm. Initial advancement was expected to be swift for the individual. There were five basic levels. New personnel typically started at the bottom, were expected to master that role within 12–18 months, and after two to four years as a junior be promoted to senior positions. At the senior level, advancement became more difficult.

Employees at Excellence were constantly evaluated. This evaluation was organized into two main processes. First, employees were evaluated in relation to their individual development. This process was labelled A-sheeting (A stands for appraisal) and carried out three to four times every year. Second, employees were ranked by their superiors in a process labelled banding. Banding occurred once a year and influenced salary level. Excellence invested heavily in the training and development of individual employees via courses, competence development groups, workshops, inviting speakers, and providing publications to those who were interested. Junior consultants were also paired with a senior consultant, who operated as a counsellor.

However, the people interviewed had experienced many deviations from the espoused ideals and ambitions of the HRM system. Good evaluations did not necessary provide a good ranking. They sometimes concluded that someone's place in the hierarchy may not reflect competence ('How in hell could he get that position?'). Organizational politics may then be more important for promotion than performance. A meeting on promotions that we observed indicated very strong politics at play as all those present tried to promote their own candidates, departed freely from the criteria set out, and invented new, sometimes metaphorically rich motivations for why their candidate alone should be promoted ('He can walk on water'). These may have been common and reasonable as overall, pragmatic HRM considerations, but whether this served the firm better than trying to maximize the ideal of meritocracy and attempting to reward and promote people based on their competence and performance is hard to say.

What makes this case more than a breakdown in understanding and *moves it to a mystery* (*step 3*) is the striking fact that organization members did *not* share the world-weary view of the HRM systems presented above. Actually, all of our informants tended to think that the HRM system did deliver. Even dissenters appeared convinced that the HRM system worked, to the extent that they tended to blame it for converting people into corporate clones. There was a widespread belief that the corporate system for selection, ranking, development and promotion was reliable, and that the resulting hierarchy expressed valid differences in technical and managerial competence. The elaborated formal differentiation system was assumed to register the actual competence of the employees:

> The Excellence brand stands for professionalism. It means that I'm serious and professional in my work. I must confess that I like the aura of the Excellence brand. I know that I was recruited to an elite and that I am still considered to be worthy of an organization that recruits the best students, has the best clients, and makes a lot of money. We hire one out of every hundred people who apply for work here. We have long and trying tests and evaluations and I have passed them all. Excellence is successful. We have passed ThinkIT as the most attractive employer among students at this country's leading business school. (Consultant)

To *elaborate and resolve the mystery* (*step 4*) of this faith in the HRM system we had to *re-imagine* (high-commitment) *HRM as an identity-aligning project.* As such it worked as a major linking mechanism between organizational identity and individual identity regulation (see also Covaleski et al., 1998). It meant organizational identity writ small – claims about what the organization stood for were here expressed in a clear, distinct, and coherent way. From this point of view it became easier to understand the widespread cognitive dissonance on HRM matters at Excellence: why the people there tended to cover up and rationalize discrepancies in the HRM system. There was simply too much at stake – the motives and social mechanisms tended to privilege positive meanings and save identity (at organizational and individual levels). In this sense, the HRM system was partly secured through the social psychology of a self-serving bias (Babcock et al., 1996; Sedikides et al., 1998).

The frequent HRM activities linked ideas about the organization and the individual – they provided points and mechanisms of identification, where organizational identity and cultural ideas became manifested and attached to the identity constructions and aspirations of the individuals. It was the investments, focus, activities, meanings, and values and not the quality and precision of all the HRM that appealed to people and made them stick with a somewhat naive belief in it. With this belief in HRM followed confidence in the firm and in themselves as carefully selected, developed, and promoted persons. HRM had then become an ingredient in the story-telling of excellence – and in this light reality tests mattered less. Where an outsider would see discrepancies in HRM practices, the insider experienced the discrediting of an integrated system of faith. In this sense the HRM system employed organizational identification through the embedding of employees within the organizational community (Scott & Lane, 2000). Excess ceremoniality fueled and expressed organizational identity and made it possible for people to retain their faith despite their experiences of HRM practices deviating from the plan. The fusion of identity and HRM made questioning the latter an unwelcome option – it would also have implied a questioning of oneself and an undermining of vital resources for identity constructions.

More generally speaking (thus *developing the resolution of the mystery* and aiming for *step 5*), the HRM system not only embedded stakeholders within the organizational community, it was also highly involved in constituting the community, in terms of the construction of the organization and individual identity projects. This, in combination with the ubiquitous and all-embracing framing of HRM practices as

ILLUSTRATING THE DEVELOPMENT AND RESOLUTION OF MYSTERIES

identity-regulating tools (feedback systems and sessions, competence development programs, promotion, and so on), made the prescribed 'reality' signified by the HRM system far more plausible and pervasive than the run-ins organizational members had with actual HR reality – with its share of weak feedback, the porosity of competence claims, and ambiguous and politicized promotions. Because HRM as a system and policy were strongly communicated in the organization and people's individual experiences of practices were not (they were hesitant in raising skepticism), these experiences tended to be compartmentalized and carried less weight for beliefs than the prescribed and publically communicated HRM 'reality'.

HRM systems and rituals thus symbolized a kind of rationality that made compliance the only reasonable response. This encouraged a leap of trust that is called for in settings in which there are no proofs or solid experiences indicating what to expect from the future (Möllering, 2001). This allows people to rationalize their position in a system that may appear old-fashioned – particularly in the professional sector – in terms of the formal hierarchy and a preoccupation with rules, standards, and titles. The Excellence people used this symbolism to help construct a positive, secure view of themselves as well as their organization. This meant that (inter-)subjectively gratifying meanings rather than observations, reasoning, and reflection guided construction processes. When fused with and in a sense 'subordinated' to (a key aspect of) organizational identity – who we are – HRM is then not subjected to 'reality tests' (critical scrutiny) in the same way that may be at play with issues that are less close to a sense of who we are (I am).

Summary

In this chapter we have provided three examples of a mystery creation and solving approach. As there are no empirical projects that we know of that have used this methodology explicitly and provided sufficient background information of the process, we have drawn upon our own research to illustrate the general relevance of our approach. The studies included here have appeared in leading journals and we would refer the reader to the full articles for further details, although the methodologies in these are not expressed in the ways used in this book, as we partly developed and conceptualized the research process afterwards, inspired by what we had found.

There are significant similarities between the cases above, but also some important differences. The cases are similar in the sense that they demonstrate that rich and nuanced data facilitated the construction of compelling mysteries, although the reported newspaper meeting draws less clearly on the broader ethnographic work of which the focused study was a part. With thinner and weaker empirical support, it is often difficult to know what to do with this, and there are more uncertainties than a case for a distinct, well grounded mystery. It is easier and more tempting to explain away any breakdowns, thus never being able to make a credible case for a genuine mystery. The cases are also similar in the sense that they not only challenged expert views, but also seemed to vex common sense. Ad agencies are not generally viewed as hot spots of machismo displays; regular meetings between senior managers are normally expected to have some impact on the shape of things; there seems to be something not quite wholesome about the rock-like belief in the good and reliable outcomes of the HRM system as clung to by the organizational members at Excellence.

However, there are some differences apparent as well. In all of the cases, the mystery was constructed by showing that the extant literature was found lacking in providing the answers that would undo the breakdown. In the third case, however, the mystery lay not only in the extant literature but also in the mystifying beliefs held by the people under scrutiny. Here, people had a strong faith in a system that frequently deviated from how it was expected to work, as viewed by the people involved. It does make sense to view some mysteries as mainly conceptual, as in the first two cases, and some mysteries as also adding a phenomenological quality, as in the third case. Working actively with informants – opening up their experiences of dilemmas and incoherencies, trying to encourage them to see things as artificial and problematic (Could one imagine doing things very differently? Does what you do here really make sense?) and other encouragements to defamiliarize them – could lead to phenomenological mysteries, which could then feed into the more theoretical mysteries that are a main interest from a research point of view.

Having said that, it seems that our suggested methodology works for both types of mysteries. In this sense, the methodology can be viewed as a generic way of tackling mystery detection and construction. Finally, although the logic of presentation forces us to present the application of the methodology as a step-by-step manual that suggests linearity and certainty, expect the business of mystery construction to be messy, non-linear, and iterative. Mysteries are carefully and painstakingly crafted and cultivated, bred by inspiration and serendipity, and should not only be understood as artefacts of rigorous and systematic method. In presenting results, a compromise between signalling something of the former and being clear, pedagogical, and economical in the text is normally necessary.

6

FIELDWORK TECHNIQUES AND MYSTERY CREATION[1]

In this book we don't really systematically or broadly address the level of fieldwork – methods for data collection, as some would put it – although we do occasionally touch upon it. As previously stated our methodology is generally compatible with all sorts of work with empirical material, and we have exemplified the overall approach with studies using experiments and questionnaires in the first chapter, and mainly interview-based and ethnographic investigations in our more detailed examples later in the book. One can, in principle, do the empirical work in conventional ways in terms of specific research practices and then add on the mystery approach at the interpretive level, as and when appropriate. One can also conduct a series of interviews or do a questionnaire and then scrutinize the results for potentially interesting deviations from what would be theoretically expected.

However, the mystery approach benefits from processual research, in the sense of studies where research questions and their design are not fixed from the beginning, but there is a possibility of and interest in seeing what emerges and being open to following unexpected results and letting these guide further empirical work. When unexpected results emerge (are creatively constructed) it is often important to let these guide a follow-up inquiry as the original research question and design (including the interview schedule or set of themes for exploration) would probably not lead to sufficient empirical material focusing on the new, emergent research interest. Follow-up investigations are often vital in order to check that the breakdown is not just as a result of limited inquiry and also in order to pick up more clues on

---

[1]Some parts of this chapter are partly based on Alvesson (2003, 2011).

how to 'solve' the mystery. Here qualitative research often has an advantage. We should not, however, overestimate this, nor see all qualitative work as being beneficial in relationship to the mystery methodology. A set of interviews carried out before a deeper analysis without any chance to come back and do follow-up interviews based on the new and unexpected ideas that have emerged, is not necessarily an advantage compared to a questionnaire for example. As the Hawthorne studies (mentioned in Chapter 1) partly showed, a set of experiments, gradually adjusted towards emergent results, may also be useful, although in the Hawthorne research subsequent qualitative work proved important. In addition it is sometimes not necessary or that helpful to 'collect' and process additional empirical work in a second stage, as a rich original set of empirical material may be sufficient for the formulation as well as for solving the mystery.

However, a process-oriented and flexible research design is still an advantage in most cases, typically but not necessarily implying qualitative research. A mixed-method study including qualitative ingredients may also be beneficial. And the opportunity to mobilize those studied in a broader and richer way than is the case in experimental and questionnaire-based research often has advantages as well. The dependence of most quantitative studies on a specific set of hypotheses and sometimes problems for understanding deviations from these in the results is at odds with a mystery approach that is actually built around the opposite ideal of these deviations being a chance to develop something new. Once again, one should not overemphasize the advantages with a qualitative approach in the context of the methodology proposed in this book, but one can still see some implications for fieldwork in qualitative research if the mystery methodology were to be used.

We therefore chose to comment upon the interview as a specific method in relationship to our overall methodology and use this to exemplify how thinking about research practices can occasionally be shown to be more in tune with a mystery approach. We will also briefly touch upon observations, mainly as something that can supplement interviews, but the bulk of our argument revolves around the interview. As qualitative researchers we also find it natural to connect to fieldwork issues in the qualitative tradition. We have addressed ethnographic work in various places in the main text. Interviews and observations are an important part in ethnographic work, although ethnographic studies will also typically include other ingredients, such as an extended period of fieldwork and an interest in cultural analysis.

We will comment in particular on how the research interview may be considered in a somewhat different or supplementary way if the researcher is more interested in working with mysteries than in emphasizing descriptive purposes. We can see some opportunities to think about interviews in a more 'mystery-compatible' way than is common, although it is fully possible to follow conventional routes for interview research and then marry these with the framework for idea and theory generation as proposed in this book.

Interviews: Conventional Views

Pierre Bourdieu, in a famous lament, once claimed that social science was cursed with talking objects. We would sometimes share his frustration but this makes it possible to use the interview as a research tool and mobilize the intellectual qualities of those being studied. Hyperbole excluded, we think it is productive to point at two dominant positions on interviews in the social and behavioral sciences. The *neo-positivist* position views interviews as an instrument for reflecting the truth about reality 'out there' through following a research protocol and getting responses that are relevant to it, while minimizing researcher influence and other sources of 'bias'. Here, 'the interview conversation is a pipeline for transmitting knowledge' (Holstein & Gubrium, 1997: 113). The *romantic* position, advocating a more 'genuine' human interaction, believes in establishing a rapport, trust, and commitment between interviewer and interviewee, and based on that, exploring the inner world (meanings, ideas, feelings, intentions) or experienced social reality of the interviewee. Through talk produced in the interview situation, the researcher becomes able to accomplish a meaningful understanding of the interviewee and his/her social world. The typical ambition of interview-studies is to accomplish 'deeper, fuller conceptualisations of those aspects of our subjects' lives we are most interested in understanding' (Miller & Glassner, 1997: 103). The romantic may be a phenomenologist, an interactionist, or another kind of interpretivist. Most of the literature on interviewing deals at length with how this practice may be utilized as effectively as possible, although sometimes doubts regarding the rationalization potential are also expressed in literature aiming to maximize the research potential of interviewing, through establishing a 'rapport', and getting the interview subject to talk a lot – openly, trustfully, honestly, clearly, and freely – about what the researcher is interested in. While realizing the complexities involved, most writers on interviews assume that skills may be developed and an approach taken in which errors are minimized and qualified empirical material will be produced etc. (see, for example, Fontana & Frey, 1994; Kvale, 1996).

The development of the interview method has moved from neopositivist conceptions to an increased awareness of the complexity of the interview situation, including the need to get full cooperation from interviewees. Most of the literature on interviewing still deals at length with how this practice may be used as effectively as possible and with how to get interview subjects to talk a lot – openly, trustfully, honestly, clearly, and freely – about what the researcher is interested in. Increasingly, however, authors will include remarks signaling caution: for example, they will use expressions such as interviewees 'reported such feelings' (Martin et al., 1998: 449) or 'gave me this account' (Barker, 1993: 408). Still, such qualifiers will only marginally soften the impression of the data and results presented as being robust and authoritative, and the reader is not encouraged to reflect upon what these accounts are really about. The interview then appears, on the whole, as a valid source of knowledge production, although it is indicated that the social process and local conditions need to be appreciated and actively managed by the interviewer in order to accomplish valid results. The purpose is to capture people's experiences or insights about reality and to use the interviews primarily for descriptive accuracy.

Considering Problems with Conventional Understandings of Interviews

Nevertheless, there are some serious problems with the conventional use of interviews that cannot really be avoided through making interview work as 'rational' as possible – in this context also including getting the interviewee to be equally authentic, truthful, and open. Problems can be seen here in the context of the typical purpose of interviews to get empirical material that says something accurate about either social reality out there (decisions, village life, etc.) or subjective meanings (values, intentions, ideas about immigrants, or a political party). As we will come back to, interviews may be used for other purposes. Of course interviews in themselves are not problematic, but it is vital to consider the risks of over-relying on interview accounts when making specific claims about how people really think or experience reality, or what this reality 'objectively' looks like.

Problems then emerge in the context of the various uses of interview material for making different kinds of empirical claims. Interviews lend themselves to being managed only to a modest degree and all such efforts will create unforeseen side-effects. There are always sources of influence in an interview context that cannot be minimized or controlled. There are also problems/complexities going far beyond what may be seen as pure 'errors'. Here we will not refer to the critique emerging from neo-positivist writers worried about 'objectivity', replicability, theory-data compatibility, and so on. (As discussed in earlier chapters, these virtues are fundamentally problematic in social sciences, e.g. Alvesson & Deetz, 2000.) What is more novel, interesting, and well informed is the critique emerging from 'qualitative' researchers who are typically interested more in social process and language use than in the traditional qualitative concerns of meaning and experience associated with the 'natives' point of view'.

Some critics, inspired by ethnomethodology, conversation and discourse analysis, emphasize that interview statements must be seen in their local, situation-specific context. In interviews, people are not reporting external events but producing situated accounts, drawing upon cultural resources in order to produce morally adequate reports. Against the neo-positivist and to a considerable extent also the romantic views on the interview as a technique for revealing reality 'out there' or people's inner lives (experiences, meaning), critics see it as local accomplishment (Silverman, 2006). As expressed by Potter (1997: 147) 'social structure becomes part of interaction as it is worked up, invoked and reworked'. At heart, the interview is a social performance. As developed in Alvesson (2011) there are several aspects of the interview that need to be taken into account to properly understand what might be going on in an interview. The interview is a complex social situation where the interview is perhaps less characterized by simply reporting facts or experiences through the use of language, and more by being engaged in complicated interactions, bearing the imprints of a multitude of social elements.

One can ask a skeptical question – what do interview accounts actually say that is more than how people talk in interviews? What is the logic behind this talk? The eight metaphors for the interview situation suggested below all represent different understandings of interviews and involve a rather basic critique of the dominant views on the subject matter (Alvesson, 2011). These proffer reconceptualizations with wide-ranging implications for interview-based research. Each involves a key feature of an interview and a central problem (challenge) that the interviewee must 'solve' or relate to:

1 The social problem of coping with an interpersonal relation and complex interaction in a non-routine situation – interview accounts then are a situation-specific response in a conversation with a specific interviewer. This is the key point of localism. Here an interview is a *local accomplishment*.
2 The cognitive problem of finding out what it is all about (beyond the level of the espoused) – interview responses reflect the interviewee's more or less accurate assumptions about what the project's purpose and researcher's intentions are. The interview is then about the interviewee *finding a story-line*.
3 The identity problem of adapting a self-position which is contextually relevant (and/or comfortable for the interviewee) – here the interviewee may wish to use the interview situation to express a specific self-image. The interview is then a site for *identity work*.
4 The 'institutional' problem of adapting to normative pressure and cognitive uncertainty through mimicking standard forms of expression – interviewees are politically correct or guided by conventions for how one should speak. What follows and an *application of scripts* for how to talk about phenomena (leadership, diversity, ethics) then dominate the situation.
5 The problem (or option) of maintaining and increasing self-esteem that emerges in any situation involving examination and calling for performance (or allowing esteem-enhancement to flourish in the situation) – the interviewee then talks very positively about him-/herself to provide a favorable view. The interview is then *impression management*.
6 The motivation problem of developing an interest or rationale for active participation in the interview – the interviewee may have hidden motives for the talk produced, perhaps serving his/her interest (possibly for the benefit of the unit or organization). This means that the interview is viewed as *political action*.
7 The representation/construction problem of how to account for complex phenomena through language – accounts then reflect problems in crafting a coherent response rather than providing a rich picture of the world 'out there'. The interview as a *crafting exercise* then illuminates what may go on.
8 The 'autonomy/determinism problem' of a powerful macro-discourse operating behind and on the interview subject – the interviewee may come across in a particular way as the theme of the interview means that they adapt to and subordinate themselves to the norms for how one should be (as an ecologically conscious consumer, professional, woman, etc.). The interview setting then expresses the *powers of discourse* that are operating on the subject.

These eight metaphors or images of the complexities and logics involved in the production of interview talk together point at a range of uncertainties concerning how to relate to interview accounts. Considering the relevance and interpretive powers of these understandings before deciding on how interviewee statements should be assessed and used could be one way of dealing with interviews in an ambitious and informed way. This obviously will have impact on how carefully one should think about what the interview generates. It becomes an open issue about what interview accounts actually say.

Using Interviews for Idea-Generation: The Interviewee as a Mystery-Seeker

What has all this to do with our proposed view of good (interesting) social science constructing and solving mysteries? The more complex understanding of interview material suggested encourages a much more sensitive social constructionist perspective on interview material than would be common. The ambiguity and openess of the material are underscored. This is in line with our overall emphasis on how we always construct empirical material. This material is, in non-trivial cases, more complicated and ambiguous than it would appear. This suggests a downplaying of the strong reliance on 'grounded theory' and more space for an imaginative openness about how to use empirical material. Thus the interview can be viewed productively as a method for generating empirical material that offers a variety of lines of interpretation. This means a multitude of potentially interesting interpretations where one or two (or even more) may kick back against the researcher's and the research field's assumptions, thereby creating breakdowns and potential candidates for mysteries. Recognizing the futility of many conventional research tasks, and asking questions that simply can't be answered – like people's 'true' values, motives, and intentions beyond just talking about these – through empirical inquiry, may trigger a re-orientation of research. All of the proposed metaphors offer potentially interesting ways of using the material. Interview material may, for example, throw light on vocabularies of motives (Mills, 1940), or identity work, or a presentation of the self as expressed in interview situations and similar social encounters (Alvesson, 1994).

Apart from opening up a broader spectrum of interpretation possibilities – not just of the reality 'out there' and the meanings of those being studied, but also of what actually goes on in the interview situation – the understanding of interviews proposed here can also suggest a relaxation of the conventional view on the use of interviews. This is typically about description, based on the assumption that through the interview guide and/or skillful flexible interviewing people are tapped for information and the set of interviews will then offer a robust ground for a valid account of the phenomenon being studied. But an empirical focus and the intention to use interviews for description can be challenged by an ideal of using interviewees as a way to find mysteries. This can of course also be done through ambitious description, but rather than being worried about precision in the validity and reliability as part of producing an empirically robust study, research interested in developing new ideas and theory will have other priorities.

This view of interviews indicates a somewhat different understanding of the interview situation and how one relates to the interviewee. Rather than being a fact-reporter or a discloser of inner life (authentic experiences), the interviewee is supposed to aid more directly the process of coming up with surprising findings. S/he can be mobilized through motives such as curiosity or an intellectual interest in research or, more generally, by a better understanding of the subject matter being investigated. The analytical capacities of the interviewer are then put more centre stage. Kreiner and Mouritsen (2005) refer to the analytical interview as different from the descriptive one. Various tendencies to go beyond the latter are also to be found in certain ideas about the interview as the co-construction of knowledge (Holstein & Gubrium, 1997). We would, in following the imperatives of the mystery idea, go further than that here. One can ask an interviewee about pointing at unexpected and curious phenomena. Within the area of interest, one can also ask about what has surprised them in terms of events or patterns, or any deviations from what one would expect based on mass media reports, theories, and the frameworks learned in school and higher education. The interview is then mobilized as a process of not just reporting how things are, but more as one coming up with empirical material that may call for a rethink of taken-for-granted assumptions or textbook knowledge. All of this is perhaps easier in studies of vocational, workplace-based or other 'expertise' areas (like political life, when politicians or journalists are interviewed). But also, when it comes to parenthood, unemployment, gender relations, being an immigrant or welfare or health care client, someone retiring, etc., one can at least with some resourceful interviewees (verbal, open, intellectual, reflective) imagine these not just for responding to questions in a researcher-led inquiry, but also for addressing people with a reservoir of observations, insights, and reflections that can aid the researcher in finding breakdowns and perhaps mysteries. Of course, what may be breakdowns for interviewees may not be so for the researcher, in a theoretical context, but the idea here is that the mobilization of the interviewee as a fellow mystery detector may aid the overall research project.

One could then do interviews partly or mainly for other purposes than producing valid descriptions. This would perhaps not typically mean a totally different interview from those oriented towards empirical precision. Some ingredients of description may be part of the interview. Interview material would nevertheless not be primarily or only targeted towards getting empirical material that was as exact or grounded as believers in the knowledge- and understanding-transmitting capacity of interviews would suggest, but would give more space for the idea-generation that is possible in (and not just through, or based on) interviews. A possible metaphor for this interview could be the interview as a mini-seminar for idea-generation.

The primary aspect of a good interview would then not be whether it captures the phenomenon being addressed in a 'correct' way, but if it shows the capacity to trigger a rethink and creativity on behalf of the researcher (the research project). The emphasis here is moved away from descriptive precision and onto idea-generative power.

But Don't Forget Descriptive Value Altogether

A change in emphasis from description to idea generation and/or analysis does not mean that the interview should not be considered exclusively in terms of the latter. Some criteria for what is a valid claim with some empirical bearing could preferably be employed. To repeat one of our key points: the idea of the mystery approach as developed here is that it should have some empirical support and that the empirical inspiration should be reasonably credible. This means a lowering of demands compared to descriptive work – where the empirical value is a key part – and also much less of a focus on the detailed codification of data as emphasized by grounded theory, but it does not imply an 'anything goes' approach. A generative or illustrative use of empirical material should be able to demonstrate that this seems to be sufficiently anchored. Empirical material as the critical dialogue partner should not be too thin and neither should it be used in a highly speculative way.

One key point then is to still think through what the empirical material is about, primarily in the context of what new ideas can be generated through questioning established assumptions and theories, and secondarily also in terms of what is a credible use of this. Given what has been addressed above as 'problems' and complications in the interview context, a crucial methodological question is to determine the basic character of specific empirical material and to what purpose it could be used. There are no good or bad methods, only good and bad ways of using material. If one is interested in saying something on a specific theme, it is crucial that the empirical material really does say something on this. So if one wants to study gendered power relations in a marriage, then interviews should be shown to be about this, and if this can't be demonstrated, then the study could be switched to show how people for example follow social scripts for talk about gender, i.e. if one can make a credible case for script application being in operation in the interview talk. (In a worst case, one may suspect that the interview talk differs significantly both from actual gender relation in the marriage and from how people will talk about the topic in other social situations, making the empirical material rather useless.) Vital to this exploration of a particular empirical material is considering two angles: interview accounts and the contingencies affecting these. Let us for example consider this in relationship to the politics of the interview account. From the first angle, the researcher may see more or less clear signs on political action in the interview account, i.e. the 'truths' may be interpreted as beneficial to the interviewee and/or his/her group, profession, or organizational affiliation. From the contingency angle, the inclination to engage in political action during the interview may be more or less profound, depending on various contingencies: the topic at stake; its perceived value and interest for the interviewee; his/her identification with, and loyalty to, the institution being studied; his/her reading of the research project and its possible outcomes, etc. It is difficult here to gain firm knowledge on these aspects, but intelligent estimations are always helpful and one may also search for supplementary evidence (observations, interviews with people that can be informed but are neutral in relationship to the issue at stake). Both content and contingency aspects need to be considered: political interests may not necessarily be explicitly manifested, but might still call for considerable scrutiny in order to be detected. At the same time, contingencies may not be apparent. Indications of a political interest-bias in an interview account may trigger a more careful evaluation of the political interest and the motives within the themes of an interview.

A Note on Observations

Observation as a technique for generating empirical material is often described as participant observation (e.g. Spradley, 1980), i.e. the researcher observes a naturally occurring event (a social setting or activity) or follows (shadows) people of interest over a certain length of time. Very ambitious observational work may be part of an ethnography, but here we must concentrate on the observation as such, i.e. without addressing the complexities of a 'full' ethnography, or going into the problems and possibilities of being a 'participant'. However, one may note that, as is often argued in the anthropology literature, researchers are at best tolerated, and are more likely to be viewed as an amusing distraction than as participants (c.f. Czarniawska, 1998; see also Kunda's (1992: 234) account of being viewed as 'overhead' for the group he studied).

Observations may appear as one way to gain a more direct and unmediated access to reality – to observe how things 'really are'. However, the romantic ideal, as discussed above, is also sometimes problematic for observations, although normally not to the same extent as for interviews. When a researcher is doing observations, the people under study may engage in various behaviors that have been triggered by their awareness that they are under scrutiny. They may also be eager to try to satisfy what they may think is the researcher's interest. For example, a family researcher observing a family may encourage them to believe this is more 'family-like' behavior than they would normally produce. Or alternatively the observer's gaze may have a disciplinary effect. A school class when studied may be less unruly because someone is sitting with them taking notes.

Having said all this, observations will typically follow different logics from interviews. The former will usually mean a much lower degree of researchers directly producing results when compared to interviews where the questions asked will produce the empirical material. The observer will be mainly inactive/refrain from interventions, while the interviewer's interventions will be framing and triggering interview responses. Observations will typically unfold in a naturally occurring context, in contrast to the 'artifact-by-research' nature of interviews. We will return to this but first we wish to say something about what observation is and how it can be done. Almost anything social can be observed, as something social by definition must happen between people. In reality, however, most observations will tend to focus on various forms of not too sensitive interactions, although individual behaviour can also be observed. Observations will typically home in on meetings, gatherings, events – any kind of human congregation that is socially legitimate. (Observing bank robbers, sexual intercourse, or harassment is often difficult.) But observations can also be framed around other phenomena. One can observe particular people, objects, processes, and spaces. One can shadow a person at work or when shopping, when they are alone or in interactions, one can observe families in interaction on buses or sitting in restaurants, all the while making notes on this.

To engage in the practice of observation – to observe – sounds easy (if a bit boring) to the uninitiated. As anyone who has actually practised observational research can attest, the boring bit is correct but the easy bit is not. It is surprisingly demanding to be denied the basic human right of being recognized by other human beings both by design and default. When doing observations this happens by design because the researcher is anxious not to interfere and thus contaminate what is going on, and by default, since most of the time the actual participants don't know why the researcher is there in the first place, they will rarely care about this anyway.

Still, observations are worthwhile despite the fact that they sap researchers' energy, and take up valuable time and resources. After all, they do provide empirical material on naturally occurring phenomena (at least roughly and for part of the time) and the material is typically extensive and rich in detail and meaning. In this sense, observations are helpful in generating the kind of empirical material we think is useful for challenging the conventional wisdom. As noted by Van Maanen (1988), this richness allows for the representation of observations and encounters in various ways that may in themselves be resources for theorization. In this sense, and others, observational material is also helpful in generating the kind of empirical material we think is useful for challenging the conventional wisdom – thick, grounded, equivocal, and so on.

Generally speaking, observational material is vital for casting light on practices and discourses in social settings. If carried out longitudinally, observations can also be instructive in revealing particular patterns of meanings, although the latter will often call for some interview work and/or a good background knowledge of the setting or community studied. In this sense, observations will complement interviews and vice versa. As mentioned, observations are less prone to the biases incurred by the problem of coping with an interpersonal relation in a non-routine situation, since the researcher is less likely to have a dominant presence in observed events, and the cognitive problem of figuring out what it's all about is probably less of an issue for most participants being targeted for observation, at least if the researcher can be vague about this and/or do observations over a longer time period. Experience indicates that those studied soon get used to and are less influenced by the observer's presence. Norm-following and expressions of self-esteem are likely to be exercised, but will have more of the character of data than of distortion. Observed behavior may reflect norms in operation and impression management as part of the everyday setting rather than the possibility of more unorthodox versions appearing in the interview setting. Motivational and representational problems would probably abound, but also present as 'interesting material' rather than as problematic distortions of truthful representation. Macro-discourses are likely to be as problematic as ever, but once again it is more interesting for most researchers to study how they can produce power effects in the settings intended for study rather than in the interview scene. In the end, it is important to emphasize that observational material expresses patterns of social conduct, while individual intentions and meanings are more accessible (or less inaccessible) in interviews. For the latter, more economical access is provided by interviews. Interviews can offer rich material, but the complexities mentioned earlier need to be carefully considered. In this sense, observations and interviews are fruitful to use in combination: observations for the establishment of actual practices and conduct, and interviews for commentary, fantasy, and clues as to what is not being directly manifested in behavior and interaction.

Compared to interviewers, researchers doing observation cannot mobilize subjects directly as participants in the search for mysteries. One can hardly ask or encourage those studied to behave in such a way that the researcher's expectations and framework are challenged. In a sense one can only hope for the best, but sometimes finding an interesting observation outlook or focus may be beneficial. One does not have to be conventional, but instead approach the site in novel ways. Actively endeavoring to construct what is happening not in line with standard categories but in unconventional ways may be helpful here. In the comparison and often confrontation between interview statements and observations one can often unearth valuable input for exploring incoherencies, contradictions, ambiguities, and other materials, which can then allow for the construction of any breakdowns and – in later stages – mysteries. This is not to say that interview talk and social practices will always or even normally be incoherent, but that the variety of material seldom encourages thinking and ideas that may deviate from neatly ordered social patterns and so this can be inspirational for the mystery-seeking researcher.

Summary

In this chapter we have addressed issues around how to address specific methods. The mystery approach can be combined with any 'data collection' method, although the flexibility of qualitative methods is an advantage. We have focused on interviews as a method where an interest in mystery-creation can motivate some revisions when compared to more conventional views. The latter typically means a focus on description – accuracy in getting the empirical material right is a priority. This is also something crucial for dataistic methods aiming to produce theory, like grounded theory which assumes that theory can be discovered through grounded data. The mystery method is based on less faith in the robustness of data and a stronger emphasis on being imaginative and rethinking established frameworks in order to come up with new ideas and theories. This means that the interview becomes interesting as an idea-generator. The interview can potentially be addressed as supportive of mystery-creation and perhaps also of mystery-solving. Surprising observations, new ideas and insights then mean more than empirical precision alone. The metaphor of the interview as a mini-seminar can support this thinking.

The more interesting the theoretical idea, the less important the amount of 'evidence' for the idea, but as said the latter is still far from unimportant in our approach. A reasonably (rather than the optimal) high degree of rigor and trustworthiness on the descriptive side is still called for, at least if the researcher aims to say something that has at least some degree of empirical support. There is always a balance here and any theoretical idea that is not extremely general and abstract will benefit from some empirical grounding, while the latter has some role to play in mystery-creation based on studies using empirical material as a critical dialogue partner.

7

RESEARCH GUIDED OR ASSISTED
BY MYSTERY?

In this book we have advocated the use of empirical material as input for theorizing in a quite different way than is common. Put succinctly, our approach encourages researchers to actively work with, expand, and vary their interpretive repertoire by being open towards and focusing on breakdowns in understandings. Breakdowns, in most research, are seen as a nuisance – they indicate that the researcher is not in control and may obstruct the research design and threaten the production of predictable results. Students interested in 'leadership', for example, may face settings in which people do not seem to be concerned about, or will refrain from/fail to produce, strong asymmetrical relations and coherent behaviours fitting into a 'leadership style' concept. Such experiences will typically not make the conventional student of leadership happy. From the approach suggested here, which is in line with a long tradition of scholarship (e.g. Becker, 1996), breakdowns are potentially good news – they may make space for theoretical reconceptualizations and development.

Breakdowns offer a vital step in the production of a mystery, but as we have already indicated many and indeed most will have limited theoretical potential. Many will be valuable primarily for their ethnographically thick description. Some will have further theoretical potential. Establishing a mystery offers an interesting source for further thinking, as it encourages problematization and self-reflexivity. This may in itself be an important contribution. But the formulation of a mystery also gives an impetus for solving it and thus for adding new knowledge beyond that of critical questioning (Asplund, 1970). This means the accomplishment of a theoretical contribution. Solving the mystery means it becomes more understandable: it is less puzzling, less ambiguous, and we will have concepts, a line of reasoning, a metaphor, or other tools which will give us a sense of what to expect and how to intellectually understand the mystery. It is seldom a matter of solving something definitively and for good. In social science there is almost never a distinct, clear, and objectively formulated problem to which a particular solution can be proposed. It is not like the relationship between avoiding lung cancer (stop smoking) and an illness caused by a bacterial infection (take antibiotics). It is always about offering new ideas, concepts, interpretations, and lines of reasoning that can credibly be shown to throw some light on the mystery and which seem to have a broader theoretical value for our thinking about a specific subject matter. Often these will be targeted by challenges and reinterpretations. Perhaps new mysteries – or the reformulation of older ones – will involve the empirical inspiration to radically rethink earlier efforts to solve mysteries.

The approach suggested here departs radically from positivistic and neo-positivistic ideas, that also characterizes a lot of qualitative research, emphasizing rationality, rigour, control, theory-data separation, and abstraction (e.g. Eisenhardt, 1989; Glaser & Strauss, 1967; Yin, 1984). It is in line with interpretive approaches, broadly defined, and emphasizing values like intuition, curiosity, problematization, openness, creativity, and challenging ideas. As Astley (1985) and Weick (1989) have pointed out, ideas picked out as inspiring and valuable by the research community are typically not characterized by a strong proven theory-data fit. After all the positivism critique of recent decades, it is time to be more bold in terms of how to interact with and creatively use empirical material. This seems reasonable, given that data are increasingly seen as constructions, emerging within a particular discourse, and impregnated by the vocabulary and line of interpretation that the researcher uses.

A mystery will emerge as a combination of the researcher's pre-understanding, including access to theoretical framework(s) and vocabularies, and the inspiration of empirical material. The ratio of input from empirical experiences against the intellectual-creative work necessary to construct a mystery may vary. Since this is a book emphasizing empirical work and methodology, we have devoted much of our attention to the role of empirical studies in triggering a mystery, but as mentioned previously 'pure' empirical impressions do not lead us very far. In addition, creativity and the concentrated supplementing of theoretical work are necessary in order to assess whether the mystery-candidate is fruitful enough for theoretical development, i.e.

is not just a breakdown for the researcher only and/or within a narrow scholarly tradition. A mystery promising a theoretical contribution must meet suitably high criteria – it can't be solved through a literature search, and calls instead for innovative theoretical work. The researcher needs to demonstrate the mystery, to empirically and theoretically make a convincing case for why it is credible, interesting, and has theoretical potential. The successful solving of a mystery means that one produces a theoretical understanding that a) illuminates the phenomenon leading to the breakdown and subsequently mystery, and b) allows for an abstracted set of ideas and concepts with broader bearing on how to make sense of similar phenomena in other settings. This does not prevent the 'solving' being, and it typically will be, partial, preliminary, and contestable.

The suggested methodological principle implies the use of a fairly open approach, where the ambition to produce a rich, multi-faceted case study and to follow up unexpected phenomena means that the research does not restrict itself to a strict *a priori* defined theme for study. Of course there will be an initial interest, but no specific ideas on how to investigate and guide the study from the start. Alternatively, the researcher will start with a specific line of inquiry but will keep their eyes and ears open and devote some of their energy to complementing a predefined line of inquiry with open themes, such as interview questions of the type 'What would be the most peculiar or interesting aspect of this setting or group of people?'. The research is much more processual and emergent than what would be typical. It would usually be ethnographic, e.g. the researcher being there for some time, coming close to everyday life, and with some interest in its meaning (Prasad, 1997; Wolcott, 1995).

However, interview-based research, documentary analysis, or even quantitative studies could also lead to breakdowns. An example of quantitative studies producing a breakdown, and briefly mentioned in Chapter 1, is Lincoln and Kalleberg's (1985) piece on job satisfaction and organizational commitment among US and Japanese workers. To reiterate, the result showed higher scores for the former, which certainly was surprising. The 'mystery' can possibly be solved through seeing questionnaire responses less as objective measurements of objective phenomena and more as clues to cultural norms for expressions and the following of language rules (Alvesson & Deetz, 2000). In general, however, the more processual, open, and empirically varied and rich a study, with the ethnography scoring best in this respect, the more likely it will be that an interesting mystery, via breakdowns, will

RESEARCH GUIDED OR ASSISTED BY MYSTERY?

be produced as well as solved. An interesting research question may be crafted based on the productive encounter of the researcher's qualified preunderstanding and the empirical material combined with further reflection and theoretical work triggered by a breakdown in understanding. The qualified surprise which indicates that established knowledge is insufficient or misleading and that also qualifies for something appearing as a mystery will mark the really interesting research questions – thereby triggering a challenge to develop something novel.

Of course all this calls for a sophisticated preunderstanding and theoretical work during the initial stages of the research process to check that this is a true mystery, and not just a surprise of very limited relevance, tied to a narrow space and place, and/or to narrow mindedness or a lack of familiarity with the relevant literature. Empirical impressions, broad scholarship, and creativity in how the empirical material can be constructed and reconstructed are necessary here, in order to produce the interesting mystery. A part of the research design then is typically (re-)consulting the literature at the right stage(s), which includes going from breakdown to mystery. One can also do follow-up interviews with subjects in order to access some assistance with insights, ideas, test interpretations, etc. after a mystery has been created and when the researcher needs additional help in order to throw light on it (Jackall, 1988; Kreiner & Mouritsen, 2005).

Many (seemingly promising) breakdowns may not lead to sufficiently interesting surprises, so the hunt for a sufficiently strong surprise offering a mystery-candidate may need to continue. A rather long exploratory phase will sometimes characterize the research project. The length of this is partly an outcome of how well one has picked and secured in-depth access to the domain of study, which is partly a matter of the researcher's skill and creativity. There is always a considerable element of chance and serendipity. At a certain time the research project will then move from being exploratory to becoming focused of developing a theoretical understanding of the empirical phenomenon (construction) which is viewed as a challenge to the established thinking. The mystery-creation (discovering/construction) work will then differ from the mystery-solving stage.

Although we think the approach developed in this book is a fruitful and under-utilized way of developing more novel interpretations of empirical phenomena and innovative theoretical ideas – and most people would probably agree there is a shortage here – some (self-reflexive) words of caution are necessary at this point. The maximalist version sketched out above is not a low-risk strategy. Constructing and solving a mystery calls for a fortunate combination of inspiring empirical material, access to a rich framework and resources for reflexivity about how to use these, creative construction work and, in the available literature, empty space for a theoretical contribution. Many research projects will have other agendas and/or will not lead to the discovery/construction of great mysteries with a strong theoretical potential.

The Use of Breakdowns in Conventional Approaches

However, more moderate uses of the breakdown idea are also possible. One alternative to a full-scale mystery-scanning research is to conduct a more conventional study, with a specific research question and a design for studying it, and to have the mystery-approach as a side project. Rather than to try to cover broader terrain and expose oneself to breakdowns, the researcher will aim primarily for control and focus, but still be open to surprises and if – indeed often when – these occur will then pursue these as partial projects. The final outcomes can thus be a variety of elements consisting of something planned and predictable, and something unexpected and perhaps more novel. In reality, such a blend of planned and emergent elements in research is common in qualitative research and one can have this as a deliberate strategy, working with a safe and another more risky aspect of research. Here, the (main) research design is fairly conventional, but there is an openness to taking breakdowns leading to mysteries seriously.

Arguably, all research approaches will confront (or will have the potential to construct) breakdowns, as long as we accept that social reality is not fully understood. (Even a strict hypothesis-testing study will typically find that some hypotheses can not be verified by data.) There is always some deviation from what a qualified researcher would expect, at least if the person does not favor a 'rubber theory' capable of explaining everything (and then typically predicting nothing). It is possible to imagine a variation in emphasis on elements of breakdowns and mysteries in research. We would propose a spectrum that includes breakdown-focused, breakdown-sensitive, and breakdown-considering research, with varying degrees of interest in and attention paid to exploring and exploiting breakdowns.

Breakdown-*focused* research means working in line fully with the ideas suggested here, aiming for a full-scale mystery-scanning approach and being more than willing to explore and construct breakdowns. The researcher must start with a fairly broad and open approach and ask such questions as 'What goes on here?' or 'What do the natives think they are up to'? One hopes to run into something unexpected and promising, using interpretive principles such as those described in Chapter 3. Of course, sometimes this intention will not be fulfilled and the research project may turn into something else. Breakdown-*sensitive* research will have a strong to modest interest in potential mysteries. It may be carried out as part of a more conventional study, which will be guided by a specific research question and a design for studying it. In this case the mystery-approach will operate as an additional guiding principle. The researcher must be open to the possibilities of an unanticipated theme and be keen to follow such themes, even when this is not the initial or primary intent of the study. Possible outcomes could be the refinement of a theory or suggestions about new lines of inquiry. The breakdown-*considering* researcher will be less inclined to work actively with breakdowns and mysteries, unless s/he bumps into something really interesting. S/he will have some awareness of the possibility of taking advantage of breakdowns, but will take this road only when extraordinary opportunities emerge. For researchers and research projects guided by this orientation, breakdowns will only play a significant role occasionally in accounting for results. When this happens, self-critique and new research questions are more likely to be the result than the formulation and solving of a mystery. However, occasionally a researcher who is initially not very breakdown-oriented may encounter breakdowns that will trigger a radical rethink. In some cases, like the Hawthorne studies mentioned in Chapter 1, the researcher will have no choice, as the hypothesis will turn out to be totally wrong and the results will be able to be 'constructed away' so that a breakdown is avoided. (Here we can say that without using the breakdown 'positively', the entire project will face a breakdown in the word's sense of falling to bits.)

Presumably, most researchers will have such a breakdown-considering research orientation, although it is difficult to find examples of researchers actually espousing it explicitly, at least in management and organization studies. The norm seems to be that the researcher will be in control – producing a linear, coherent study, where research questions, framework, fieldwork, empirical results and conclusions that will follow a rational procedure. Even in some research drawing upon Foucauldian and other poststructuralist ideas, the studies reported tend to produce conventional 'depersonalized, third-person and apparently objective and authoritative representations' (Wray-Bliss, 2002:

QUALITATIVE RESEARCH AND THEORY DEVELOPMENT

20; see also Richardson, 2000). This may say more about the established standards for presentation in journals – despite decades of positivism-critique – and less about how researchers actually work. Arguably, breakdowns and projects following these are not so rare, but there may be a need to make them more legitimate and explicit.

Which methods are most suitable for research working with breakdowns and mysteries? As explored in earlier chapters, with a somewhat different emphasis, we have two answers here. The first is that the more a study is processual, emergent, open, and empirically varied and rich, the more likely it is that an interesting mystery, via breakdowns, will be produced and in particular solved. Ethnographic studies (Brewer, 2000; Wolcott, 1995), as well as more conventional interview-based research, have some advantages here. Other studies which are open to the views of research subjects (perhaps seeing them as co-participants; see Heron, 1981; see Kreiner & Mouritsen, 2005), and allowing them to express unconstrained voices in the research, may also increase the frequency of breakdowns appearing. Combining methods (like interviews and observations) can offer interesting discrepancies between talk and practices (which can lead to interesting questions). Our second answer – and this is our main point – is that all kinds of research can lead to, or be used for, the discovery or construction of breakdowns and mysteries. As our initial reference to Lincoln and Kalleberg (1985) and the Hawthorne studies indicated, even questionnaire studies and experiments may provide interesting breakdowns. The Hawthorne studies are particularly illuminating in this respect, as the researchers encountered completely unexpected findings that then made it necessary to rethink the entire project from scratch. The ideas discussed here are thus of a potential broad relevance, even though research that does not allow for the flexibility of developing and exploring new ideas in the process of getting additional empirical material may have difficulties in *solving* a mystery. Often, however, the formulation of a mystery can be a huge contribution: it can be a vital step in encouraging reflexivity and new lines of inquiry. Asking innovative questions can be just as important as providing answers.

In addition to being feasible in any kind of research, breakdowns can in principle occur at almost any point in the research process, based on serendipity or conscious efforts to reflexively remain open to breakdowns occurring. Working with empirical material in different phases is noteable here. The trend of a shifting emphasis from fieldwork towards text-work (Geertz, 1988; Richardson, 2000; Van Maanen, 1988) has pointed to the importance of writing in crafting ideas and articulating findings. One can also start the research process by problematizing the assumptions within a specific literature in order to reduce its grip and the inclination that follows to construct empirical material in a pre-given way (Alvesson & Sandberg, 2011). Our approach does not necessarily imply a linear development. We indicated earlier the potentially cyclical nature of this kind of research. Breakdowns and mystery construction may begin with the writing process, which then may lead the researcher to return to field notes or other empirical material (interview protocols, questionnaires), to the literature, or even to go back to the field for a follow-up study. The kind of curiosity and willingness to reconsider the received wisdom that characterizes the research methodology suggested here is thus not limited to a specific phase in the research project.

Conclusion: Breakdowns, Mysteries, and Dialogues

As the literature on the interplay between theory and empirical material is vast and varied, it is difficult to claim that our contribution is in all respects a great invention. Rather we would synthesize, expand, sharpen, and refine ideas that to a degree have already appeared in social science. We would also add new conceptualizations. But compared to what is common and dominant in the research methodology – which typically circulates around a so-called rigorous treatment of data – our suggested methodology is clearly different and offers an alternative.

We can distinguish between three elements in our contribution:

1 Our first contribution concerns the introduction and to some degree the development of a general framework for and an alternative conceptualization of the research process. The aim primarily is not to provide a blueprint for methodology, but to offer inspiration through a guiding set of generative ideas. We have advocated a framework for thinking about empirical material and how this can be used in more creative and challenging ways than may be common. This means going beyond recommending openness and following where the data may lead us, while meantime actively working with alternative constructions. One aspect here is encouraging a willingness to be surprised in research and to also be willing to revise the frameworks and traditions from which one originates. Not just encountering but also trying to *produce* breakdowns is a vital part of this approach, in which problematizing existing ideas is crucial. The challenge is to surprise oneself by rather than control the empirical material. The view of empirical material

QUALITATIVE RESEARCH AND THEORY DEVELOPMENT

as a critical dialogue partner rather than as a signpost or as a validator of truth claims is important here.

2 A second and somewhat more specific contribution concerns vocabulary which has been touched upon in the previous paragraph. We can capture the advocated alternative conceptualizations through metaphors and we have used both critical and positive ones. Conventionally data are seen as building blocks in research, as unknown territory (of facts and/or meanings) to be discovered and/or judged in terms of what are true/valid and false/non-acceptable claims to knowledge. We are skeptical of metaphors such as data guiding or ultimately validating theory. Empirical materials are, in most cases that are of interest to the social studies, not robust, but are shaped and reshaped in various ways depending on the language and perspectives used. We would propose alternative metaphors and conceptualizations. Empirical material would be seen as a potential dialogue partner, leading to questioning, doubting, and problematizing the existing/dominant expectations and frameworks. Theory would be viewed as a potential tool for disclosure. So too would be breakdowns in understanding. We would suggest the creation and solving of mysteries (aided by breakdowns) as a root metaphor for the research process. We would also suggest that concepts such as sensitive constructions, interpretive repertoires, and reflexivity could be helpful in realizing the full generative potential in breakdowns and mysteries.

3 A third contribution here concerns the specific methodology proposed for working with breakdowns and mysteries. We hope this is not to be read as a recipe, and would argue that in an area of methodology where 'progressive' (e.g. constructivist) ideas are frequently rather abstract and of uncertain relevance to research practice that outlining a research process which takes these ideas seriously may be supportive. There is a strong norm of presenting research results in a fairly linear and rational way. Researchers have difficulty in fully using constructivist ideas in empirical studies and will take the insight about the fusion of theory and empirical material seriously. We have formulated an alternative to dominating and sometimes misleading notions of research as a mainly rational process of planning, execution, and analysis based on a separation of theory and data and the minimization of researcher subjectivity. We have suggested five interpretive principles ((de)fragmentization, problematization, defamiliarization, broad scholarship, and reflexive critique). We have also proposed a model of the research process consisting of five steps. These two elements of the overall methodology are loosely related and will structure the work differently. The methodology is very flexible, as indicated by breakdown-focused, breakdown-sensitive, and breakdown-considering research.

For a believer in conventional methodology, including the most popular versions of qualitative methods, this may appear a dangerous and unreliable enterprise. But a similar critique can be directed at hypothesis-testing and inductive projects that will frequently exhibit a misleading rigour and robustness. As the purpose is to generate new ideas, it is important that we do not emphasize rigor too much and that we give space to the researcher's imagination when working with empirical material. With a realization of the role of language and social construction in subjects and institutions 'out there' (targeted for study) and also within academia, even the seemingly most robust and rational of enterprises, rigor, and the delivery of unproblematic objective results will become open to doubt. Still, we are not propagating an 'anything goes' version or a licence for researchers to be creative and try to innovate for the sake of saying something novel. Researchers need to persuade the skeptical reader: to build a convincing case involving illuminating empirical material, using a well-mastered interpretive repertoire, and demonstrating elements of reflexivity in the process, as well as adopting a careful and sophisticated understanding of the relevant literature. In the end, this is no less demanding than building a theory from the data gathered or validating and falsifying hypotheses.

This book suggests a general attitude to and an alternative conceptualization of the research process. Its aim is not primarily to provide a blueprint for methodology, but instead to offer a source of inspiration through a set of generative and inspiring concepts. We can capture this alternative conceptualization via the use of metaphors. Conventionally, data can be seen as building blocks for research, as unknown territory to be discovered, and/or judged in terms of what is true/valid and false/non-acceptable claims to knowledge. This chapter proposes metaphors of empirical material as a potential dialogue partner, a source of questioning, doubt, and a problematization of existing/ dominant expectations and frameworks. As a critical dialogue partner, empirical material does not just express a distinct voice, its mobilization is also an outcome of the questions asked, the perspectives involved, the various framings and re-framings of the issues at hand. The dialogue setting (involving a researcher's preunderstanding, an alternative theoretical input, and empirical material) forms an interactive whole. Breakdowns in understanding mean opportunities for learning and knowledge creation. Some of these learning opportunities will be more tied in with understanding the local field; others may lead to more radical, theoretical reconceptualizations. The creation and solving of mysteries thus become general guiding metaphors for the research process.

The approach suggested here gives considerable space to the researcher's subjectivity – their preunderstanding, imagination, feeling for what is interesting – at the expense of plans, procedures, and techniques. The latter is in many cases of great importance, but in research aiming at developing ideas these are not to be privileged. Working with mysteries calls for much more than rationality and rigor. But as has been stated, researcher subjectivity needs to be cultivated and disciplined. And rather than delivering knowledge that gives priority to reliability or validity – or even to plausibility – it should be strongly biased in favor of interesting, challenging, and novel ideas.

Arguably, the social sciences need much more of this. With an increasing pressure to publish journal articles and the strong tendency for these to adapt to a conventional format and to satisfy expert reviewers who are often heavily involved in a subfield where they wish to accept map-the-gap logic and piecemeal contributions to existing literature, we will get narrow and often uninteresting research. This book tries to make a modest contribution to a quite different idea within social science. Here the detective novel forms a more inspiring model than the idea of gap-spotting and gap-filling. To take earlier research and theory as a starting and reference point is fine and necessary, but often really interesting research doesn't so much proceed and build on it than problematize and rethink part of it. As we have tried to show, empirical studies and material can be mobilized for the benefit of this project.

REFERENCES

Abbott, A. (2004) *Methods of Discovery: Heuristics for the Social Sciences*. New York: Norton.

Agar, M. (1986) *Speaking of Ethnography*. Thousand Oaks, CA: SAGE.

Alvesson, M. (1993a) *Cultural Perspectives on Organizations*. Cambridge: Cambridge University Press.

Alvesson, M. (1993b) 'The play of metaphors'. In J. Hassard and M. Parker (eds), *Postmodernism and Organizations*. London: SAGE.

Alvesson, M. (1994) 'Talking in organizations: managing identity and impressions in an advertising agency', *Organization Studies*, *15*: 535–563.

Alvesson, M. (1998) 'Gender relations and identity at work: a case study of masculinities and femininities at an advertising agency', *Human Relations*, *51* (8): 969–1005.

Alvesson, M. (2002) *Postmodernism and Social Research*. Buckingham: Open University Press.

Alvesson, M. (2003) 'Beyond neo-positivists, romanticists and localists: a reflexive approach to research interviews', *Academy of Management Review*, *28* (1): 13–33.

Alvesson, M. (2010) *Interpreting Interviews*. London: SAGE.

Alvesson, M. and Billing, Y.D. (2009) *Understanding Gender and Organization* (2nd edn). London: SAGE.

Alvesson, M. and Deetz, S. (2000) *Doing Critical Management Research*. London: SAGE.

Alvesson, M., Hardy, C. and Harly, B. (2008) 'Reflecting on reflexivity: reappraising reflexive practice in organisation and management theory', *Journal of Management Studies*, *45* (3): 480–501.

Alvesson, M. and Kärreman, D. (2000) 'Taking the linguistic turn in organizational research: challenges, responses, consequences', *Journal of Applied Behavioural Science*, *36* (2): 134–156.

Alvesson, M. and Kärreman, D. (2007) 'Creating mystery: empirical matters in theory development', *Academy of Management Review*, *32* (4): 1265–1281.

Alvesson, M. and Sandberg, J. (2011) 'Generating research questions through problematization', *Academy of Management Review*, *36*(2).

Alvesson, M. and Sköldberg, K. (2009) *Reflexive Methodology* (2nd edn). London: SAGE.

Alvesson, M. and Sveningsson, S. (2003) 'The good visions, the bad micro-management and the ugly ambiguity: contradictions of (non-)leadership in a knowledge-intensive company', *Organization Studies*, *24* (6): 961–988.

Ashcraft, K.L. (2000) 'Empowering "professional" relationships: organizational communication meets feminist practice', *Management Communication Quarterly*, *13* (2): 347–392.

Ashcraft, K.L. and Mumby, D. (2004) *Reworking Gender*. Thousand Oaks, CA: SAGE.

Asplund, J. (1970) *Om undran inför samhället*. Lund: Argos.

Astley, G. (1985) 'Administrative science as socially constructed truth', *Administrative Science Quarterly*, *30*: 497–513.

Babcock, L., Wang, X. and Loewenstein, G. (1996) 'Choosing the wrong pond: social comparisons in negotiations that reflect a self-serving bias', *The Quarterly Journal of Economics*, *111*: 1–19.

Barker, J. (1993) 'Tightening the iron cage: concertive control in self-managing teams', *Administrative Science Quarterly*, *38*: 408–437.

Barlebo Wenneberg, S. (2001) *Socialkonstruktivism*: *Positioner, problem och Perspektiv*. [Social Constructivism: Positions, Problems, and Perspectives.] Malmö: Liber.

Barlow, G. (1989) 'Deficiencies and the perpetuation of power: latent functions in management appraisals', *Journal of Management Studies*, *26* (5): 499–517.

Bärmark, J. (1999) 'Forskningspsykologi [Research psychology]'. In C.M. Allwood and M. Erikson (eds), *Vetenskapsteori för psykologi och andra samhällsvetenskaper*. Lund: Studentlitteratur.

Becker, H. (1996) *Tricks of the Trade*. Chicago: The University of Chicago Press.

Berger, P. and Luckman, T. (1967) *The Social Construction of Reality*. New York: Anchor.

Boween, D. and Ostroff, C. (2004) 'Understanding HRM-firm performance linkages: the role of the "strength" of the HRM system', *Academy of Management Review*, *29* (2): 203–221.

Brewer, J. (2000) *Ethnography*. Buckingham: Open University Press.

Broms, H. and Gahmberg, H. (1983) 'Communication to self in organizations and cultures', *Administrative Science Quarterly*, *28*: 482–495.

Brown, R.H. (1977) *A Poetic for Sociology*. Chicago, IL: University of Chicago Press.

Brunsson, N. (1985) *The Irrational Organization*. Chichester: Wiley.

Burrell, G. and Morgan, G. (1979) *Sociological Paradigms and Organisational Analysis*. London: Heinemann.

Butler, J. (2004) *Un-doing Gender*. London: Routledge.

Calás, M. and Smircich, L. (1992) 'Re-writing gender into organizational theorizing: directions from feminist perspectives'. In M. Reed and M. Hughes (eds), *Re-thinking Organization: New Directions in Organizational Theory and Analysis*. London: SAGE.

Calás, M. and Smircich, L. (1999) 'Past postmodernism? Reflections and tentative directions', *Academy of Management Review, 24* (4): 649–671.

Charmaz, K. (2000) 'Grounded theory: objectivist and constructivist methods'. In N. Denzin and Y. Lincoln (eds), *Handbook of Qualitative Research* (2nd edn). Thousand Oaks, CA: SAGE.

Cockburn, C. (1991) *In The Way of Women*. London: Macmillan.

Covaleski, M. et al. (1998) 'The calculated and the avowed: techniques of discipline and struggles over identity in big six public accounting firms', *Administrative Science Quarterly, 43*: 293–327.

Czarniawska, B. (1998) *A Narrative Approach in Organization Studies*. Thousand Oaks, CA: SAGE.

Davis, M.S. (1971) 'That's interesting! Towards a phenomenology of sociology and a sociology of phenomenology', *Philosophy of the Social Sciences, 1*: 309–344.

Deetz, S. (1992) *Democracy in an Age of Corporate Colonization: Developments in Communication and the Politics of Everyday Life*. Albany: State University of New York Press.

Deetz, S. (1996) 'Describing differences in approaches to organizational science: rethinking Burrell and Morgan and their legacy', *Organization Science, 7*: 191–207.

Deetz, S. (1997) 'The business concept and managerial control in knowledge-intensive work: A case study of discursive power'. In B. Sypher (ed.), *Case Studies in Organizational Communication*. New York: Guilford.

Deetz, S. (1998) 'Discursive formations, strategized subordination, and self-surveillance: an empirical case'. In A. McKinley and K. Starkey (eds), *Foucault, Management and Organizational Theory*. London: SAGE. pp. 151–172.

Delanty, G. (2005) *Social Science* (2nd edn). London: SAGE.

Denzin, N. (1994) 'The art and politics of interpretation'. In N. Denzin and Y. Lincoln (eds), *Handbook of Qualitative Research*. Thousand Oaks, CA: SAGE.

Denzin, N. and Lincoln, Y. (1994) 'Introduction: entering the field of qualitative research'. In N. Denzin and Y. Lincoln (eds), *Handbook of Qualitative Research*. Thousand Oaks, CA: SAGE. pp. 1–17.

Denzin, N. and Lincoln, Y. (2000) 'Introduction: the discipline and practice of qualitative research'. In N. Denzin and Y. Lincoln (eds), *Handbook of Qualitative Research* (2nd edn). Thousand Oaks, CA: SAGE.

Denzin, N. and Lincoln, Y. (2005) 'Introduction: the discipline and practice of qualitative research'. In N. Denzin and Y. Lincoln (eds), *Handbook of Qualitative Research* (2nd edn). Thousand Oaks, CA: SAGE.

Deutsch, F.M. (2007) 'Undoing gender', *Gender & Society, 21* (1): 106–127.

Dingwall, R. (1997) 'Accounts, interviews and observations'. In G. Miller and R. Dingwall (eds), *Context & Method in Qualitative Research*. London: SAGE.

Ehn, B. and Löfgren, O. (1982) *Kulturanalys*. Lund: Liber.

Eisenhardt, K. (1989) 'Building theories from case study research'. *Academy of Management Review, 14*: 532–550.

Fontana, A. and Frey, J. (1994) 'Interviewing: the art of science'. In N. Denzin and Y. Lincoln (eds), *Handbook of Qualitative Research*. Thousand Oaks, CA: SAGE.

Foucault, M. (1980) *Power/Knowledge*. New York: Pantheon.

Freese, L. (1980) 'Formal theorizing', *Annual Review of Sociology, 6*: 187–212.

Garfinkel, H. (1967) *Studies in Ethnomethodology*. Englewood Cliffs, NJ: Prentice-Hall.

Geertz, C. (1988) *Work and Lives: The Anthropologist as Author*. Cambridge: Polity.

Gergen, K. (1978) 'Toward generative theory', *Journal of Personality and Social Psychology, 36*: 1344–1360.

Gergen, K. and Gergen, M. (1991) 'Toward reflexive methodologies'. In F. Steier (ed.), *Research and Reflexivity*. London: SAGE.

Gioia, D. and Pitre, E. (1990) 'Multiparadigm perspectives on theory building', *Academy of Management Review, 15*: 584–602.

Glaser, B. and Strauss, A. (1967) *The Discovery of Grounded Theory: Strategies for Qualitative Research*. Chicago, IL: Aldine.

Goffman, E. (1959) *The Presentation of Self in Everyday Life*. Garden City, NY: Doubleday.

Gregory, K.L. (1983) 'Native-view paradigms: multiple cultures and culture conflicts in organizations', *Administrative Science Quarterly, 28*: 359–376.

Habermas, J. (1972) *Knowledge and Human Interests*. London: Heinemann.

Hardy, C. and Clegg, S. (1997) 'Relativity without relativism: reflexivity in post-paradigm organization studies', *British Journal of Management, 8*: S5–S177.

Hassard, J. (1991) 'Multiple paradigms and organizational analysis: a case study', *Organization Studies, 12*: 275–299.

Hearn, J. (1993) 'Emotive subjects: organizational men, organizational masculinities and the (de)construction of "emotions"'. In S. Fineman (ed.), *Emotions in Organizations*. London: SAGE.

Heron, J. (1981) 'Experiential research methodology'. In P. Reason and J. Rowan (eds), *Human Inquiry: A Sourcebook for New Paradigm Research.* Chichester: Wiley.

Hollway, W. (1984) 'Gender difference and the production of subjectivity'. In J. Henriques et al. (eds), *Changing the Subject.* London: Methuen.

Holstein, J.A. and Gubrium, J. (1997) 'Active interviewing'. In D. Silverman (ed.), *Qualitative Research.* London: SAGE.

Jackall, R. (1988) *Moral Mazes.* New York: Oxford University Press.

Jaggar, A.M. (1989) 'Love and knowledge', *Inquiry, 32*: 151–176.

Jeffcutt, P. (1993) 'From interpretation to representation'. In J. Hassard and M. Parker (eds), *Postmodernism and Organization.* London: SAGE.

Kanter, R.M. (1977) *Men and Women of the Corporation.* New York: Basic.

Kärreman, D. and Alvesson, M. (2001) 'Making newspapers: conversational identity at work', *Organization Studies, 22*: 59–89.

Keenoy, T. (1999) 'HRM as hologram: a polemic', *Journal of Management Studies, 36*: 1–23.

Kincheloe, J. and McLaren, P. (1994) 'Rethinking critical theory and qualitative research'. In N. Denzin and Y. Lincoln (eds), *Handbook of Qualitative Research.* Thousand Oaks, CA: SAGE.

Knorr-Cetina, K. (1994) 'Primitive classification and postmodernity: Towards a notion of fiction', *Theory, Culture & Society, 11*: 1–22.

Kreiner, K. and Mouritsen, J. (2005) 'The analytic interview'. In S. Tengblad et al. (eds), *The Art of Science.* Malmö: Liber.

Kuhn, T.S. (1970) *The Structure of Scientific Revolution.* Chicago: University of Chicago Press.

Kunda, G. (1992) *Engineering Culture: Control and Commitment in a High-Tech Corporation.* Philadelphia: Temple University Press.

Kvale, S. (1996) *Interviews.* Newbury Park, CA: SAGE.

Lakoff, G. and Johnson, M. (1980) *Metaphors We Live By.* Chicago: University of Chicago Press.

Leach, E. (1982) *Social Anthropology.* Glasgow: Fontana.

Leidner, R. (1991) 'Serving hamburgers and selling insurance: gender, work, and identity in interactive service jobs', *Gender and Society, 5* (2): 154–177.

Lewis, M. and Grimes, A. (1999) 'Metatriangulation: building theory from multiple paradigms', *Academy of Management Review, 24*: 672–690.

Lincoln, Y. and Guba, E. (2000) 'Paradigmatic controversies, contradictions, and emerging confluences'. In N. Denzin and Y. Lincoln (eds), *Handbook of Qualitative Research* (2nd edn). Thousand Oaks, CA: SAGE.

Lincoln, J. and Kalleberg, A. (1985) 'Work organization and workforce commitment: a study of plants and employees in the US and Japan', *American Sociological Review, 50*: 738–760.

Locke, K. and Golden-Biddle, K. (1997) 'Constructing opportunities for contribution: structuring intertextual coherence and "problematizing" in organizational studies', *Academy of Management Journal*, 40 (5): 1023–1062.

Lyotard, J.-F. (1984) *The Postmodern Condition: A Report on Knowledge*. Minneapolis, MN: University of Minnesota Press.

Marcus, G. and Fisher, M. (1986) *Anthropology as Cultural Critique*. Chicago: University of Chicago Press.

Martin, J. et al. (1998) 'An alternative to bureaucratic impersonality and emotional labour: bounded emotionality at the Body Shop', *Administrative Science Quarterly*, 43: 429–469.

Melia, K. (1997) 'Producing "plausible stories": interviewing student nurses'. In G. Miller and R. Dingwall (eds), *Context & Method in Qualitative Research*. London: SAGE.

Merton, R.K. and Barber, E. (2004) *The Travels an Adventures of Serendipity: A Study in Sociological Semantics and the Sociology of Science*. Princeton: Princeton University Press.

Miller, J. and Glassner, B. (1997) 'The "inside" and the "outside": finding realities in interviews'. In D. Silverman (ed.), *Qualitative Research*. London: SAGE.

Mills, C.W. (1940) 'Situated actions and vocabularies of motives', *American Sociological Review*, 5: 904–913.

Mills, C.W. (1959) *The Sociological Imagination*. New York: Oxford University Press.

Mintzberg, H. (1979) *The Structuring of Organizations*. Englewood Cliffs, NJ: Prentice-Hall.

Möllering, G. (2001) 'The nature of trust: from Georg Simmel to a theory of expectation, interpretation and suspension', *Sociology*, 35 (2): 403–420.

Morgan, G. (1980) 'Paradigms, metaphors, and puzzle solving in organization theory', *Administrative Science Quarterly*, 25: 605–622.

Morgan, G. (ed.) (1983) *Beyond Method: Strategies for Social Research*. Beverly Hills, CA: SAGE.

Morgan, G. (1997) *Images of Organisation*. Thousand Oaks, CA: SAGE.

Mumby, D. and Putnam, L. (1992) 'The politics of emotion: a feminist reading of bounded rationality', *Academy of Management Review*, 17 (3): 465–486.

Parker, M. and McHugh, G. (1991) 'Five texts in search of an author: a response to John Hassard's "Multiple paradigms and organizational analysis"', *Organization Studies*, 13: 451–456.

Peirce, C.S. (1978) 'Pragmatism and abduction'. In C. Hartshorne and P. Weiss (eds), *Collected Papers vol V*. Cambridge, MA: Harvard University Press. pp. 180–212.

Pinder, C.C. and Bourgeois, V. (1982) 'Controlling tropes in administrative science', *Administrative Science Quarterly*, 27: 641–652.

Poole, M.S. and Van de Ven, A. (1989) 'Using paradox to build management and organization theories', *Academy of Management Review*, *14*: 562–578.

Popper, K. (1963) *Conjectures and Refutations: The Growth of Knowledge*. London: Routledge and Kegan Paul.

Popper, K. (1972) *Objective Knowledge: An Evolutionary Approach*. Oxford: Clarendon.

Popper, K. (1976) 'On the logic of the social sciences'. In T.W. Adorno et al. (eds), *The Positivist Dispute in German Sociology*. London: Heinemann.

Potter, J. (1997) 'Discourse analysis as a way of analysing naturally occurring talk'. In D. Silverman (ed.), *Qualitative Research: Theory, Methods and Practice*. London: SAGE.

Potter, J. and Wetherell, M. (1987) *Discourse and Social Psychology: Beyond Attitudes and Behaviour*. London: SAGE.

Prasad, P. (1997) 'Systems of meaning: ethnography as a methodology for the study of information technologies'. In A. Lee et al. (eds), *Information Systems & Qualitative Research*. London: Chapman & Hall.

Ragin, C.C. (1987) *The Comparative Method: Moving Beyond Qualitative and Quantitative Strategies*. Berkeley: University of California Press.

Richardson, L. (2000) 'Writing: a method of inquiry'. In N. Denzin and Y. Lincoln (eds), *Handbook of Qualitative Research* (2nd edn). Thousand Oaks, CA: SAGE.

Rorty, R. (1979) *Philosophy and the Mirror of Nature*. Princeton: Princeton University Press.

Rorty, R. (1989) *Contingency, Irony and Solidarity*. Cambridge: Cambridge University Press.

Rorty, R. (1992) 'Cosmopolitanism without emancipation: a response to Lyotard'. In S. Lash and J. Friedman (eds), *Modernity & Identity*. Oxford: Blackwell. pp. 59–72.

Rosenau, P.M. (1992) *Post-Modernism and the Social Sciences: Insights, Inroads and Intrusions*. Princeton: Princeton University Press.

Sandberg, J. and Alvesson, M. (2011) 'Routes to research questions: Beyond gap-spotting', *Organization*, 18, 1: 23–44.

Schwartzman, H.B. (1987) 'The significance of meetings in an American mental health center', *American Ethnologist*, *14*: 271–294.

Schwartzman, H.B. (1993) *Ethnography in Organizations*. Newbury Park, CA: SAGE.

Scott, S. and Lane, V. (2000) 'A stakeholder approach to organizational identity', *Academy of Management Review*, *25*: 43–62.

Sedikides, C., Campbell, K.W., Reeder, G.D. and Elliot, A.J. (1998) 'The self-serving bias in relational context', *Journal of Personality and Social Psychology*, *74*: 378–386.

Shotter, J. (1993) *Conversational Realities: The Construction of Life through Language*. Newbury Park, CA: SAGE.

Shotter, J. and Gergen, K. (1994) 'Social construction: knowledge, self, others and continuing the conversation'. In S. Deetz (ed.), *Communication Yearbook 17*. Newbury Park, CA: SAGE.

Silverman, D. (2006) *Interpreting Qualitative Data*. (3rd edn). London: SAGE.

Spradley J. (1980) *Participant Observation*. New York: Holt, Rinehart, and Winston.

Steier, F. (1991) 'Reflexivity and methodology: an ecological constructionism'. In F. Steier (ed.), *Research and Reflexivity*. London: SAGE.

Strauss, A. and Corbin, J. (1990) *Basics of Qualitative Research*. Newbury Park, CA: SAGE.

Strauss, A. and Corbin, J. (1994) 'Grounded theory'. In N. Denzin and Y. Lincoln (eds), *Handbook of Qualitative Research*. Thousand Oaks, CA: SAGE.

Sutton, R. and Staw, B. (1995) 'What theory is not', *Administrative Science Quarterly, 40*: 371–384.

Thomas, J. (1993) *Doing Critical Ethnography*. Newbury Park, CA: SAGE.

Townley, B. (1999) 'Practical reason and performance appraisal', *Journal of Management Studies, 36*: 3: 287–306.

Tsoukas, H. (1991) 'The missing link: a transformational view of metaphors in organizational science', *Academy of Management Review, 16*: 566–585.

Van de Ven, A. (2007) *Engaged Scholarship: A Guide for Organizational and Social Research*. New York: Oxford University Press.

Van Maanen, J. (1988) *Tales of the Field: On Writing Ethnography*. Chicago, IL: University of Chicago Press.

Van Maanen, J. (1995) 'An end to innocence: the ethnography of ethnography'. In J. Van Maanen (ed.), *Representation in Ethnography*. Thousand Oaks, CA: SAGE.

von Glasersfeld, E. (1991) 'Knowing without metaphysics: aspects of the radical constructivist position'. In F. Steier (ed.), *Research and Reflexivity*. London: SAGE.

Watson, T. (1994) *In Search of Management*. London: Routledge.

Weick, K. (1989) 'Theory construction as disciplined imagination', *Academy of Management Review, 14*: 516–531.

Weick, K. (1993) 'The collapse of sensemaking in organizations: the Mann Gulch disaster', *Administrative Science Quarterly, 38* (4): 628–652.

West, C. and Zimmerman, D.H. (1987) 'Doing gender', *Gender and Society, 1* (2): 125–151.

Wittgenstein, L. (1953) *Philosophical Investigations*. London: Blackwell.

Wolcott, H. (1995) 'Making a study "more ethnographic"'. In J. Van Maanen (ed.), *Representation in Ethnography*. Thousand Oaks, CA: SAGE.

Wray-Bliss, E. (2002) 'Abstract ethics, embodied ethics: the strange marriage of Foucault and positivism in labour process theory', *Organization*, 9 (1): 5–39.

Yin, R. (1984) *Case Study Research: Design and Methods*. Thousand Oaks, CA: SAGE.

SUBJECT INDEX

Macro 47, 109
Meaning 30, 38, 42, 90
Men 81
Metaphor 24, 79, 105
Methodological 106
  Principle 40, 78, 113
Micro 47
Mystery 65–6, 68, 82, 95,
    112, 117
  Approach 97–8, 105
  Creation 16, 63, 70–5

Neo-positivism 7, 15, 99–101,
    112
Newspaper, study of 84–90
Non-decision 84

Objective 20, 113
Observation 29, 59, 107–109

Perspective 36, 48
Political 62
  Action 51, 106
Positivism 4, 7, 112
Postmodernism 5
Poststructuralism 54
Power 19, 43
Practice 30, 67, 72
Pre-understanding 5, 15,
    60, 61
Problematization 15, 41
  of the taken for granted 45–7

Qualitative
  Research 10, 24, 31, 76,
    112, 115
  Study 5, 22, 79
  Work 30, 98
Quality 25, 75
Quantitative studies 20, 31, 98, 113
Questionnaire 20, 30, 113
  Research 7

Reflexive critique 41, 49–51, 69
Representation 30, 32, 108
Research 6, 17, 29, 55, 113
  Critical 44
  Cultural 44
  Design 75, 98, 114
  Interview 22, 99
  Process 68, 73, 118
  Questions 2, 97, 114, 116
  Social 25, 58, 62, 75

Script 53
Social construction 34, 103, 120
Structure 43, 67, 101
Subjectivity 54, 58, 62

Techniques 97
Theory 2, 27, 36, 58
  Development 5, 15, 17, 20, 49
Truth 7, 25, 39, 50, 106

Voice 30, 33

AUTHOR INDEX

Supporting researchers for more than forty years

Research methods have always been at the core of SAGE's publishing. Sara Miller McCune founded SAGE in 1965 and soon after, she published SAGE's first methods book, *Public Policy Evaluation*. A few years later, she launched the Quantitative Applications in the Social Sciences series – affectionately known as the 'little green books'.

Always at the forefront of developing and supporting new approaches in methods, SAGE published early groundbreaking texts and journals in the fields of qualitative methods and evaluation.

Today, more than forty years and two million little green books later, SAGE continues to push the boundaries with a growing list of more than 1,200 research methods books, journals, and reference works across the social, behavioural, and health sciences.

From qualitative, quantitative and mixed methods to evaluation, SAGE is the essential resource for academics and practitioners looking for the latest in methods by leading scholars.

www.sagepublications.com